303.484 COL
Dispatches from the
occupation : a history of
Collis, Stephen, 1965-
952831

Dispatches from the Occupation **KL NOV 2012**

MI 3/15

SI APR 2015

RU APR 2017

GO OCT 2018

SO-EJJ-302

KL NOV 2012

Also by Stephen Collis

Anarchive

*The Commons**

Mine

*On the Material**

Phyllis Webb and the Common Good:
*Poetry / Anarchy / Abstraction**

Through Words of Others:
Susan Howe and AnarchoScholasticism

*Available from Talonbooks

Dispatches from the Occupation

A History of Change

STEPHEN COLLIS

Talonbooks

Copyright © 2012 Stephen Collis

Talonbooks
P.O. Box 2076
Vancouver, British Columbia, Canada v6b 3s3
www.talonbooks.com

Typeset in Minion and printed and bound in Canada.
Printed on 50% post-consumer recycled paper.

Cover design by Typesmith.
Cover photograph by Will Winter.
Photographs on pages 72 and 90 by Brian Houle.
Photographs on pages 50, 88, and 134 by Stephen Collis.

First printing: 2012

The publisher gratefully acknowledges the financial support of the Canada
Council for the Arts, the Government of Canada through the Canada
Book Fund and the Province of British Columbia through the British
Columbia Arts Council and the Book Publishing Tax Credit for our
publishing activities.

All rights reserved. No part of this book may be reproduced, stored in
a retrieval system or transmitted, in any form or by any means, without
the prior written consent of the publisher or a license from the Canadian
Copyright Licensing Agency (Access Copyright). To obtain a copyright
license, visit www.accesscopyright.ca or call toll free to 1-800-893-5777.

Library and Archives Canada Cataloguing in Publication

Collis, Stephen, 1965–
Dispatches from the occupation : a history of change / Stephen Collis.

Includes index.
Also issued in electronic format.
ISBN 978-0-88922-695-1

    1. Occupy movement—British Columbia—Vancouver. 2. Protest
movements—British Columbia—Vancouver. 3. Social change—History.
I. Title.

HN110.V3C64 2012   303.48'40971133   C2012-903919-5

For the occupiers, everywhere

For a very long time, the intellectual consensus has been that we can no longer ask the Great Questions. Increasingly, it's looking like we have no other choice.

— DAVID GRAEBER,
Debt: The First 5,000 Years

Contents

Preface

It was, at least for me, an unexpected beginning. I heard about Occupy Wall Street (OWS) at about the same time I heard there was going to be a general assembly (GA) to discuss an occupation of Vancouver – perhaps in late September 2011. The world, it seemed, had been going through a general "loosening" of the tight wrappings round social potentiality since the beginning of the year. Tahrir Square, clearly, *meant something.* I was vaguely aware of the May 15 movement in Madrid and of the ongoing austerity-fueled turmoil in Greece. Looking back to the year before, the Toronto G20 Summit in June 2010 clearly signaled that austerity was in our future here in the "developed" world, too, as was an intense militarized opposition to dissent – the $1 billion security budget for the summit was nearly on par with security spending for the Olympic Winter Games in Vancouver earlier that year.

The Vancouver and London riots in the summer of 2011 also *meant something* – despite outraged claims in the media about their meaninglessness. "Hooliganism" and "boredom" aren't enough of an explanation – in fact they are no explanation at all. Neither is alcohol enough of an explanation. People – young people, ordinary young people – were angry as hell. They could see their prospects shrinking before their eyes, hope and possibility disappearing from the world ahead.[1] Indignation, inarticulate rage, were becoming a global phenomenon. Where were we headed?

And then, three years after the 2008 economic crash – like a delayed reaction – in lower Manhattan, we, the people, appeared to be striking back. We had something to say – in fact, a lot to say. And we had a methodology and a rallying cry.

Arriving at that first GA in Vancouver on October 8, I was already familiar with the use of hand signals and the human microphone from watching videos of OWS. I had a sense of what "occupying" meant, and who the "99%" were – or at least what this term might stand for, this new calculus of power and alienation. I had even joined Facebook for the first time, as it seemed that social media sites were where revolutions began now. I was ready for whatever happened next. Or so I thought.

In the coming days and weeks, I became increasingly involved in Occupy Vancouver. I joined the media committee[2] and began writing for the blog; made daily visits to the encampment; followed, watched, and read everything I could on Facebook and elsewhere; and attended GAs and committee meetings as often as possible. As I wrote for the blog, I did so with the people I'd met in mind, with their faces, their voices, and their words. I certainly felt like I was writing *for* the movement, channeling whatever aspect of the general intellect that I was attuned to and able to understand. I felt that I was not trying to "explain" Occupy to the uninitiated so much as I was trying to reflect back to the occupiers themselves what they were saying and doing as a way to help keep them motivated, on task, and aware of the big picture. I took the media committee's statement seriously: its task was "to function as a loudspeaker for the movement." A blog isn't exactly very "loud," but it's what I could provide.

As the weeks went by, I began to take on other roles – occasional ad hoc spokesperson, organizer, another body willing to drag and carry, march and chant. There were always people more involved than I was – people who offered more crucial day-to-day "leadership" (a role anyone, at any time, in theory could, and often did, step into as the occasion arose). I had to have some degree of "objectivity" to think carefully about what was happening, and sometimes thought of myself, half in jest, as an "embedded" academic – but I sympathized with everything the movement was trying to achieve, and increasingly the roles of "writer" and "activist" blurred and became indistinct. Happily so, I should say now. If I erred in the blogs I wrote it was probably on the side of an upbeat optimism, as I often saw my role as a motivational one.

The enthusiasm was hard to resist. Hannah Arendt, describing the *sociétés révolutionnaire* of 1789, noted their "enormous appetite for debate, for instruction, for mutual enlightenment and exchange of opinion, even if all these were to remain without immediate consequence on those in power."[3] This was what anyone who spent any time at an Occupy encampment in the autumn of 2011 could also not avoid noticing: people wanted, above all else, to learn from each other, to teach each other, to share their thoughts and ideas, to listen and to be heard. They wanted a place for this free exchange. They wanted an agora. And they still do.

★

In September 2011 I sat down to write a book about *change*. The words of the poet Charles Olson were forefront in my mind: "What does not change / is the will to change." The human being, at some deep, ontological level seemed to be a changeling, as well as a changemaker. The will – free or otherwise – would be an important part of this investigation. I intended it to be a philosophical book, and naively and idealistically planned a trip to Europe to, more or less, write about change in the midst of very old things that seemed by turns to resist and to betray a great deal of change.

Then Occupy happened. All that remains of that original book about change – something of a vestigial limb – is this book's concluding section, "Letter from Rome." The bulk of the book I *did* write – *Dispatches from the Occupation* – comprises the blogs written during the occupation, and selected essays I wrote in the months following eviction, mostly for a new website I started with filmmaker Ian MacKenzie: Occupy Vancouver Voice. This book begins with an essay assessing the Occupy movement in the context of the history of social revolutions: what is really new about it and what it owes to the past.

It is a book not so much about Occupy Vancouver specifically, but rather about the Occupy movement writ large – this moment of seemingly inexorable social change – which uses Occupy Vancouver as its immediate point of reference (for obvious reasons). It is a book integrating reportage and analysis, "news" and philosophy, poetry and political theory – the whole jumble of rants, proclamations, manifestos, thoughts, screeds, and squibs that coursed through one occupier's aching head and heart over some seven or eight months.

This book is also written on the basis of a very simple, straightforward, and I think not uncommon premise: that social, economic, and political change is absolutely necessary now, at this historical juncture. And it is premised on the notion that change is coming whether we will it or not – indeed it is upon us now – but that we might be able to collectively "will" the pace and direction of this change, how it impacts, who it impacts, and where it ultimately leads us.

This is easy enough to say, but the devil, as the saying goes, is in the details. I intend to identify many of those details in this book. I also think we need to have some understanding of *what change is* – how we have thought about it in the past and how we might contend with it now. What Occupy has put on the table is the very idea that the changes we need to make are drastic and sweeping – structural and systemic. I attempt to flesh this idea out some here, knowing others will do so, too.

As of this writing, it is June 2012. It seems that calls for a global "re-occupation" have gone by unnoticed in Vancouver and much of North America. It is easy enough to say that the Occupy movement has "failed." It has failed, in some very real internal (its ability to sustain itself as a unified movement) and external (what it has actually, materially accomplished) senses. But, I think more importantly, the new moment of social possibility and struggle for justice is just beginning, and the Occupy movement has played an important role in that opening. This book is not an autopsy of the movement; it is an exploration of this new moment the movement has opened. "The best Utopias are those that fail the most comprehensively," writes Fredric Jameson, thereby making us that much "more aware of our mental and ideological imprisonment." But in the end, Jameson concludes (ironically echoing Margaret Thatcher), "there is no alternative to Utopia."[4] We have to try, no matter how much failure is a part of our trying.

Perhaps the next stage will not involve "occupying" as we saw it in the fall of 2011, and perhaps we will not even refer to it as "Occupy" anymore (which won't be such a bad thing, considering the historical oppressions that word is freighted with).[5] One can indeed already see the rumblings of the movement's next phases, its next circuits of energy and organization. In Chicago recently, thousands marched in protest against NATO talks. In Mexico and Spain, students are organizing. In Montreal, too, tens – even hundreds – of thousands of students, who have been in the streets for months, have been joined by many others in facing down a new draconian, anti-democratic protest law, and violent police oppression – a situation that the world is now waking up to and rallying against. In Montreal, one participant offers this description, which captures what so many people have been feeling, the world over, as they have spilled into the streets to find each other over this past year.

> I wish I could properly convey to you what it feels like … It is magic. It starts quietly, a suggestion here and there, and it builds. Everybody on the street begins to smile. I get there, and we all – young and old, children and students and couples and retirees and workers and weird misfits and dogs and, well, neighbours – we all grin the widest grins you have ever seen while dancing around and making as much noise as possible. We are almost ecstatic with the joy of letting loose like this, of voicing our resistance to a government that seeks to silence us, and of being together like this. I have lived in my neighbourhood for five years now, and this is the most I have ever felt a part of the community; the lasting impact that these protests will have on how people relate to each other in the city is deep and incredible.[6]

What we seem to be witnessing now are waves of movements – rising, cresting, ebbing, and then rising again. Each building upon the one that came before – Arab Spring, *Indignado*, Occupy, Maple Spring – these waves are all part of one growing surge of change, a rising tide of opposition to the current world order. A threshold we have hovered upon for some months now – years even – may at last be in the process of being crossed. This book is written on that threshold.

Acknowledgments

The essays and blog postings in the "Dispatches" section appeared, sometimes in slightly different forms, on the Occupy Vancouver media blog, Occupy Vancouver Voice, The Mainlander, and rabble.ca.

"A Show of Hands: Art and Revolution in Public Space" began as a talk I was invited to give at the Vancouver Art Gallery, for the opening of Kota Ezawa's *Hand Vote* at the VAG "Offsite" space, February 4, 2012. Thanks to Vanessa Kwan and Kathleen Ritter. This essay was also included in *West Coast Line* 73 (Spring 2012). Thanks to Jason Starnes, David Gaertner, and Michael Barnholden.

I first presented "The Metabolic Commons; or, From Occupying to Commoning through Decolonization" at Tragedy of the Market: From Crisis to Commons, January 6–8, 2012, Burnaby, Coast Salish Territories. Thanks to organizers Fiona Jeffries, Harjap Grewal, and Harsha Walia. Excerpts from this talk were also included on the Future of Occupy website – thanks to those editors, too: Mark Jagdev, George Por, and Mary Beth Steisslinger.

I gratefully acknowledge the generous support of the Canada Council for the Arts. A Jack and Doris Shadbolt Fellowship also made the writing of this book possible: special thanks to the Faculty of Arts and Social Sciences, Simon Fraser University.

Thanks to those very politically engaged poets who have inspired and challenged me over many years now: Phyllis Webb, Roger Farr, Reg Johanson, Cecily Nicholson, Rita Wong, Larissa Lai, and Christine Leclerc.

Thanks to Ian MacKenzie, Derrick O'Keefe, and Jordan Boschman. Special thanks to all the organizers, activists, and occupiers I have worked with this past year – you know who you are, and you have taught me more than I can ever properly thank you for.

And finally, thanks to my family for supporting and understanding my need to be out and about and in the public eye so much this past year.

PART 1

REPETITION AND DIFFERENCE: OCCUPYING THE HISTORY OF CHANGE

1.

What matters is not to propose a theory of
the movement, but to show the movement in
its true character and elaborate the elements
of a theory ... A theory of the movement has
to emerge from the movement itself, for it is
the movement that has revealed, unleashed,
and liberated theoretical capacities.

— HENRI LEFEBVRE
The Explosion

We live, so it seems, under perpetually alternating weathers of
hopelessness and hope. We swing, almost imperceptibly, between
despair and distraction, between visions of destruction and
moments of soothing forgetfulness. Every day brings some new
alarm – an earthquake or a hurricane, a terrorist attack or a war –
new reports about which chemicals and which products are now
known to cause cancer, what factories are to be closed and which
workers to be laid off, what bank bailout and excessive corporate
bonuses are to be paid from the public purse, what new spate of
home foreclosures is enforced, what new genetic experiment is
finding its way into our food supply, what new last vestige of ancient
forest is to be cut, what species gone extinct, what river polluted by
the latest oil spill from a ruptured pipeline, what gulf filling with
clouds of petroleum as its last large fish die in drift nets ...

And at each new announcement of the destruction of
individuals, communities, and ecologies – the sudden intervention
of an exciting and slick new gadget that will make our lives so
much easier and richer, a new celebrity scandal, a blockbuster

movie, a new drug or product that will keep us balanced on the knife edge of health and dependence, a new mega-project to deliver jobs and prosperity to communities and economies on the edge of collapse.

It's as though these two moments – of despair and hope, of impending doom and instant mind- and soul-numbing gratification – were artfully planned for us, carefully coordinated or scripted, like a film taking us through emotional highs, lows, and highs again as it progresses through its three acts, our hearts in the director's hands throughout. To guide our emotions toward complacency and quiescence. To stall us at the point where the promise of freedom blurs into frustration.

★

We want, above all else, to change. To *be* different and to *make* a difference. To be better. Healthier. Smarter. Richer. More beautiful. More loving and loved. If only we tried a little harder, worked a little harder, we seem to think. Change – a new self, a new world – is always just there, dangling tantalizingly in front of us, just out of reach. A new, more creative, more connected, more fulfilling life. A new health regimen. A world saved for art and beauty. We think it's just a matter of our purchasing power. The corporations tell us they are ready to help: growth is the answer; buy their products and you change the world. They are "innovators," after all – change-makers. They can help unveil the new you. They can in fact help you *be* a new and better you. At least, every advertisement is there to tell us this is so, to lull, soothe, calm, coerce, and cajole us between the shock and awe of "news" and "entertainment," every day harder to distinguish.

We push on. We strive – using ourselves up, year after year. Socioeconomic prospects diminish, and our personal and national debt rises. Struggling, we console ourselves with the many available distractions. Alcohol and drugs. Food and sex. Money. Sporting events. TV. The Internet. Facebook and Twitter swallow us up into a monetized simulacrum of "the social." We forget the horrors, and the hours slip by …

But the world of frights comes back again when the distractions wear thin. Unemployment. Austerity. Environmental calamity. A seemingly unresponsive, arrogant, and inadequate judicial and political system. Something nefarious, coercive, must be at work, stacking the deck and tilting the playing field. It all seems too large and complex for any one of us to "change," despite how much we would like to change ourselves and the suffering world around us. And then the fields of distraction are there again, beckoning. We could eat. We could shop. We could go online, check our friends' status updates, their amusing and ironic posts. Anger is available, too, and there are those who readily distract us by telling us where to channel our anger, at which group, who to exclude, whose inhuman fault all this is …

Of course, the distractions are there to make money for the few who truly benefit from the excesses of consumer society. Of course, the consequences of this society – environmental destruction, chemical and electromagnetic poisoning of our bodies and minds, alienation, wasted time and lives, poverty and marginalization, violence and outright exploitation – are more than overlooked: they are depended upon, the very method of turning a profit and keeping the machinery going. Of course, that the judicial and political system only really serves the interests of capital accumulation and the 1% who run and benefit from this accumulation is simply apropos. What can you – the coerced and complacent 99% – possibly do about this all-pervasive system? Just do your job and enjoy your entertainment. Leave the big questions to the rich and powerful, the experts, and the "leaders."

★

When Barack Obama came along, we in Canada were even caught up in the enthusiasm, with the very idea that he could *bring* – that he in fact *was* – *change*. "Yes we can" – change everything, fundamentally. I was skeptical, personally. But I watched. The 2008 US presidential election made for good television, and it played simultaneously to our need for both hope and distraction. When Obama stepped onstage in Chicago after winning the election, I cried, like so many others captured by the camera's lens that night, as they stood cheering in the audience. Sweeping the history of American racism, slavery, the Civil War, and the civil rights movement up into that frenetic moment, there was the shock of realization that the president of the United States was *black*, and that this was difference, *that this was change* – visceral and visible change.

And then nothing changed. No "color-blind" society ensued. Wars went on. Poverty went on. Massive profits for banks and corporations went on. Our alienation went on. Racism, sexism, exploitation. It wasn't his fault, necessarily. If race is, ultimately, something of the surface – a social construct – then the change represented by Obama was a change of the surface. It was not change at a structural level. I imagined him as a shipmaster being led to the bridge of state for the first time, taking the wheel in his hands. And trying to turn it. It's a huge ship, already on a course long set. Obama pulls hard on the wheel, but there is no response. The ship does not turn very fast. In fact, the wheel in the president's hands seems to be a decoy – a toy wheel. Down in the engine room, the real motive force and directive capabilities are at work. Maybe he knew this all along, and dutifully played the game of decoy and puppet. Maybe it was a shock. We'll never know.

★

Are all of our hands tied? Can we do nothing? Must we sit back and watch the "civilization" we have built follow the course it has been on – a self-destructive course – or do we have the agency and willpower to stop this civilization's forward momentum, to realize its defect, and to begin again, begin anew?

Dave Meslin suggests that it is not a question of our apathy, but rather, a question of our being "actively discouraged from engagement" by a system that "constantly puts obstacles and barriers in our way."[1] The political decision-making process – at whatever level of government – is kept largely out of sight, out of mind. Most of us don't know how to engage with it (beyond the alienating and periodic voting process, which we experience much the same way we do shopping: *I guess I'll take the blue one*) – and most of the time we could care less, because there's so much to distract us from our political alienation and powerlessness.

★

Then Tahrir Square happened. It seemed beyond imagining – the citizens of a country long under military rule taking to their streets, occupying their central square, and demanding wholesale change. Make no mistake – the calls were for regime change – but this meant a great deal more than a mere change in leadership, as subsequent events have made clear (note, for instance, the fact that Egyptians were once again filling Tahrir Square, more than a year after Mubarak's ouster). The violence was incredible, but the multitude stood its ground, and much of the world kept close to their televisions and computers to watch.

The occupation of public space – the general "strike" of the public – had arisen as a new, momentous strategy. For everyone to assemble under the banner of change, putting a halt to the current system which cannot possibly continue if everyone opts out.

I took a sheet from the *Globe and Mail* and taped it to my office wall – a double-page color photograph, shot from above, of a Cairo street scene, where a sea of black-clad riot police confront a sea of multicolored demonstrators.[2] The front line, where the two forces meet, is a wall of Muslim women, haranguing the heavily armed riot cops.

I remember trying to understand who these people were. They seemed to be everyone and anyone. Young and old. Students and businessmen. Men and women. They fought and fought – and they won (more or less). I don't know that anyone could have predicted this. I don't know that anyone could not be deeply affected by this: its suddenness, its manifestation of the fact that – inexplicably – *change does still happen in this world, people still do, collectively, affect the course of history.* They rise up. They struggle for the common good.

Tunisia, of course, had preceded Egypt, and then Yemen and Bahrain followed. Dominos? A virus? Or a new social rhythm passing from smartphone to smartphone, computer to computer, making its way through the network.

Greece burned, its anarchists fighting austerity measures tooth and nail, the air filled with arcing cans of tear gas, its lines of riot cops, their clear plastic shields doused with the flames of Molotov cocktails.

In Madrid, on May 15, 2011, people took to the square once again. Many, many thousands seeming to at once materialize the processes and structures of a new society within the groaning shell of the old. Camping in tents. Holding general assemblies. They called themselves *Indignados* – the indignant. This is how revolutions begin: with the voice of honest indignation, with a beleaguered people announcing, *"Enough!"*

And then, on September 17, protestors occupied Wall Street. A wave seemed to be circling the globe. It was, above all, a wave of spontaneity, a wave of possibility, a wave of change.

On October 15, in hundreds, and soon thousands, of cities across North America and around the world, we, the 99%, the multitudes of many nations, of all races, origins, genders, faiths, and backgrounds, took our squares. In Vancouver we declared ourselves to be "a non-violent movement for social, economic, and political change," and we offered this "statement of unity":

> We humbly acknowledge that Occupy Vancouver is taking place on unceded Coast Salish territories.
>
> We, the Ninety-Nine Percent, come together with our diverse experiences to transform the unequal, unfair, and growing disparity in the distribution of power and wealth in our city and around the globe. We challenge corporate greed, corruption, and the collusion between corporate power and government. We oppose systemic inequality, militarization, environmental destruction, and the erosion of civil liberties and human rights. We seek economic security, genuine equality, and the protection of the environment for all.
>
> We are inspired and in solidarity with global movements including those across the Middle East, Europe, and the Occupy Wall Street / Occupy Together movement in over 50 cities in Canada, and

thousands worldwide. Injustice anywhere is injustice everywhere.

We are committed to an inclusive and welcoming space, to addressing issues of oppression and discrimination, and to creating an environment where all the 99% can be heard and can meaningfully participate. We are also committed to safeguarding our collective well-being – including safety from interpersonal violence and any potential police violence.

★

I think we are now at a moment to which many things have contributed. The evolution of neoliberal capitalism over the past four decades and the pressures and hardships it has forced upon the masses – building to a head in the recent financial crises, bailouts, and subsequent austerity measures. The sudden rise and disappearance of "May 1968" (and the related convergence of social movements in the 1960s) as a moment of social possibility, driven under the neoliberal waves raising only the most exclusive boats, its potentialities unresolved. The re-emergence of transnational resistance in the late 1990s anti-globalization movement, and then its partial submersion under renewed American imperial aggression – the wars in Afghanistan and Iraq – the ubiquitous "war on terror."[3] The Zapatista uprising in Chiapas in the mid-1990s, complete with a critique of neoliberalism, a renewed call for the commons, and a fascinating juxtaposition of the Internet and the jungle, social networking and masked uprising. And finally the writings of a number of key theorists of the new revolutionary moment – Michael Hardt and Antonio Negri (*Empire*), Naomi Klein (*The Shock Doctrine*), David Harvey (*Spaces of Hope*), and the Invisible Committee (*The Coming Insurrection*) among them. All these prepared the ground and set the fuse of the new explosion of global dissent – the sudden and unexpected Occupation of Everywhere in 2011.

2.

"Events upset the structures which made them possible," Henri Lefebvre writes early in his 1968 book *The Explosion*. "Movement flares up where it was least expected ... Against this background are projected new elements of social life; these now become briefly visible in luminous transparency."[4] Lefebvre wrote about the events of May 1968 – the massive student uprising in Paris and the general strike in France – in very close proximity, publishing his response before the end of the year. Everything was fresh, as yet unresolved, the ultimate outcome of "events" still largely unknown. Writing now in the first half of 2012, still only months after the beginning of the Occupy movement, I find myself in a similar position, similarly *in medias res*, and so I turn to Lefebvre as an able guide to navigating this new social formation. But more than this, May 1968, and Lefebvre's in-the-moment theorizing about its significance, has much to teach us about the events of the fall of 2011 and the ongoing, as yet unresolved Occupy movement – as the above quotation I think clearly indicates. Indeed, Lefebvre often sounds like he could be directly addressing the circumstances of this past year.[5]

However, what we now share with 1968 is as instructive as what we do not, and I will offer only a brief précis here, turning where appropriate to similar and equally enlightening comparisons with the anti-globalization movements of the late 1990s and early 2000s. The winds of social change are upon us once again; we have much to learn, in terms of *how* social change is "facilitated," as well as how it is defeated or "deflected," from these two most recent social movements that were arrayed – as we are once again, in thousands of cities across the world – to reject the current system "by struggling against it in its totality."[6]

Part of what drives us to create something completely *other than* the existing socioeconomic system is that which places us in a confrontational position *within* the existing socioeconomic system: the awareness of extreme and growing inequality, the fact that we are the 99%, waking up to the reality of the excesses of a global 1% which has amassed much of the wealth and political power in the world, and the terrible reality that the system that benefits and props up this 1% does so at the expense of the ecological commons we all – every species on this planet, in fact – depend upon. The social and ecological abuses perpetrated by the global 1% are matched by their willingness to sacrifice everything to keep this system in place as long as possible.

In this essay, I discuss a number of paradoxes or contradictions, such as those between differing strategies and tactics, which both characterize and sometimes befuddle this moment of expanding global social-movement building. My position is that the contradictions of the Occupy movement are its strength and true potential; the movement's ability to contain, and not simply to seek to resolve, these contradictions is its potentially unique contribution to the history of social movements. Ultimately, it is my argument that these contradictions are underwritten by the challenge of having to both *struggle against* the global 1% and the destructiveness of the system that keeps it in place, and, at one and the same time, to *evolve beyond* it by imagining and immediately building upon the possibilities of another world – one of greater equality, environmental stewardship, and global commoning. This is just the beginning. We are still learning how to lead our double lives of being against, and simultaneously evolving beyond, global capitalism.

ON POSSIBILITY

In many ways what was most striking for Lefebvre about the events of May 1968 was their embodiment of possibility or what I have called, in reference to the Occupy movement, a claim upon a "right to the future." What is at stake now, as in 1968, is the very idea of "tomorrow," both in terms of who will have a say in the constitution of our tomorrows, and now, especially, amid the current ecological crisis, whether we can even conceive of viable tomorrows. In 2011, what was most unexpected was the palpable urgency and sincerity of the idea that we had the *potential* to actually *change* the way things were at a very fundamental level. In this regard, Lefebvre's dialogue between a "possibilist" and "someone more practically oriented," armchair quarterbacking the revolution of '68, is highly instructive.

The possibilist notes that "the Revolution ... was there ... It only had to be seized ... The centers of production were *occupied,* so were the centers of communication ... But the attack was not made."[7] In 1968, the revolution came to the brink, but it did not go over the edge and completely transform society from the bottom up. An election was forced, and French president Charles de Gaulle looked for a moment to flee the country, but very little actually, materially changed, despite the millions who had taken to the streets in the largest general strike (and a wildcat one at that) in history. People went back to their same jobs (if they hadn't been fired). Students by and large went back to their classrooms (if they hadn't been expelled). The economy, after stuttering and sputtering, went on performing the work of capitalist accumulation.

That is what is at question in this dialogue – why did the revolution of 1968 not go all the way? With twenty-two million workers on strike, how did the working people of France not refashion their society in their own image? This is an important question for us to consider in 2012. Clearly we have not gone as far as France did in 1968 (although the Occupy movement is more widespread, if not as deeply entrenched). We have not "occupied" the centers of production and communication; we have occupied public space, generally, but that is something different. In Canada, organized labor and university students have been fairly quiet (aside from the incredible actions of students in Quebec throughout early 2012).[8] The economy has teetered, globally, on its own wobbling axis of crisis and contradiction, debt, and default – but here in Canada the left has largely played a wait-and-see game as our economy has stubbornly hung on to its (nevertheless shrinking and increasingly oil-dependent) bubble.

What has been "occupied" in 2011, I would argue, is the debate itself, the question of *what* is happening, and *what* is to be *done* –

on a global level. It has been more about ideology than material production – more, to use the old Marxist terms, about the superstructure than the base (more about this in due course). The incredible thing, the shift in consciousness, the real open door of the potential, was that so many people (even the mainstream media, to a certain extent) wanted to hear about, and talk about, broad questions of social change, whereas they had for so long turned a deaf ear and a blind eye. Social movements became *news* once again. People threw themselves into the big and vaguely defined ambitions of the Occupy movement with enthusiasm. Many others were curious, and willing to stop and debate, ask questions, and listen to what must sometimes have seemed outrageous answers. The message was clearly getting through to the vast majority of people: something was seriously wrong, and new solutions were called for. We'd seen the box. Now we wanted to hear a bit about what was outside it.

Lefebvre's possibilist sounds very much like an occupier, who has similarly been accused of being without a "plan," without clear demands, and without a vision. As the "practical-minded" interlocutor calls for "direction, orientation" and "a theory," the possibilist insists that such orientation "must be invented, created. New forms of social life" fashioned on the spot, in situ – "revolution is a process," not a program.[9] Whereas in 1968 the revolution hesitated because of, on one side, a fear that it lacked "orientation" and "a theory," and on the other, a vague commitment to an unspecified, new, and spontaneous "process," in 2011 the commitment was, from the beginning, to a "process," to a "theory," if you will, of decision making, action, and participation that would embody a new world growing in the crumbling shell of the old. It is more a question of the *form* being the *content* (and I would argue that this was adhered to, quite consciously, throughout the global occupations) than worrying, as in past decades, about what (ideologically specific) content might come to fill the new forms of direct action and "taking the square" to enact new agoras.

This is to say that the question in 1968 – how to answer "the new set of problems resulting from a crisis of institutions and from the reconstruction, not of a state, but of an entire society"[10] – is still the question in 2012. But the difference is that now we are (potentially) more prepared to answer this question – because we have, across a broad global movement, all more or less bought into the same basic strategy and template. The new process isn't entirely new anymore – it's been around at least since 1968, when it was so new as to cause a crucial, even fatal, hesitation and self-doubt, and to wither under heavy criticism from liberal and leftist power brokers (not to mention the antipathy of the right). We have learned from the past. We have tried and tested models of horizontal decision making and group dynamics (although these are of course made anew in each moment of social upheaval). Activists have been at work, behind the scenes, for years, working on the strategy that we have all seemingly spontaneously now leapt into. But more importantly, crucially in fact, the crisis has expanded in its nature: what makes this period of crisis in capitalism (2008–) different from past crises is not only its *degree* (though a globalized economy and financial system *do* make a difference), but also its being joined and inextricably entwined with the growing reality and awareness of the global environmental crisis. Now we know that we are "all in this together" – that the stakes are that large. This is what the metric of the 99% indicates. A prospering 1% is not going to "float all boats" on its rising tide; it's draining the sea itself, hoping that what puddles remain will be for its vast yachts alone.

Unlike 1968, to rise up now in Paris is also to rise up in Bangkok, Thailand; Lawrence, Kansas; London, England; and Vancouver, British Columbia, simultaneously. We now live largely networked and decentralized lives (despite the parallel structure of massive and ever-increasing centralization of power and wealth); so we can now mobilize on a scale, and with a consistency, not seen before in history. We can actually, potentially, *be* a 99% meeting and challenging a corporate-bureaucratic-military 1%, rising against it everywhere at once. However there is still so very much to learn, and we are just now flexing this new potentiality – even as the powers arrayed against us are devising new legal and lethal means to stop us.

As the Invisible Committee writes in *The Coming Insurrection* (another harbinger of the present moment, with its opening announcement, like Lefebvre's, of an imminent "explosion"), in today's world "crisis is a means of governing" as the world now "seems to hold together only through the infinite management of its own collapse."[11]

We are at a new limit (economic crisis). Capitalism's usual propensity to renew itself (via creative destruction) when it reaches such a limit is struggling in the face of the ultimate limit – the planet itself, its impact on the entire biosphere – and a growing sense, even among the economic possibilists, that the impossible, as far as growth is concerned, is finally here. "Disaster capitalism" may have met its final disaster. At least, there's an "opportunity" here, now, for either a new attempt to tear down and rebuild capitalism, or to tear down and *replace* capitalism. The debate about crisis is what is being occupied. It's a question of our social possibilities, of what we will collectively imagine and make of this moment, this opportunity.

ON SPONTANEITY

"Without spontaneity there would be neither event nor move- ment," Lefebvre writes. Spontaneity directly leads into the streets – "an area of society not occupied by institutions," and it leads, in some way, shape, or form, to "violence."[12]

Spontaneity – as opposed to, say, a carefully planned and covert putsch orchestrated by a vanguard party – was part and parcel of the "newness" of 1968, a re-emergence of what were seen as anar- chist tactics (relying as they did on the unpredictable upswelling of the very base of society, of instantly unleashed, and therefore uncontrolled, action) after years of Cold War and party politics. The events of May that year largely caught the traditional left off guard, and occurred mostly outside the space of parties and unions. Students in Paris's suburbs rose up, followed by students in the urban core (the Sorbonne), and finally organized labor's rank and file joined in (though largely against the wishes of their "organ- izers"). May 1968 was spontaneous in origin, an upwelling of anomie and indignation, as the Occupy movement has been, too.

I recall reading an article, in the summer of 2011, in which the author mused about the 2011 Arab Spring possibly migrating across the Atlantic. It seemed unlikely, and was being raised wistfully to show how sclerotic and apathetic North American society was. *Adbusters'* call for an occupation of Wall Street didn't get much media attention, and even after September 17, it was some weeks before many people outside of New York City began to take notice of what was going on – only when some seven hundred people were kettled and arrested on the Brooklyn Bridge. Then, suddenly – seemingly out of the blue – October 15 came, and occupations were launched at the centers of nearly a thousand cities worldwide.

"Spontaneity," Lefebvre writes, "holds out a magnificent vision and possibility: the total reconstruction of society, a democracy permeated by the movement, based on a network of 'base' organisms in which all interests, all aspirations and all liberties would be actively present (instead of being merely represented). This notion of a democracy rooted in the base is forcefully opposed to the notion of a republic (public thing) managed and maintained at the top."[13]

Again, this analysis applies to the Occupy movement of 2011/12 just as well as it did to May 1968. Spontaneity is part and parcel of the horizontally distributed self-governance model being employed across the Occupy movement, where it only takes the gathering together of whoever is occupying a particular space at a particular moment to start organizing, making decisions, and acting collectively.

Spontaneity is the very essence of grass-roots movements: they rise unexpectedly from below, appearing all around us and in many separate locations at once. They are characterized by a kind of impatience with the world – for good reason. The world around us – structured for very particular (and unequal) purposes (the accumulation of capital and power in very few hands) – is designed to change only slowly, and in a highly controlled fashion, if at all. "It is useless to *wait*," the Invisible Committee announces, "We are already situated *within* the collapse of a civilization. It is within this reality that we must choose sides." The implications of this urgency are becoming clear to many: "To no longer wait is, in one way or another, to enter into the logic of insurrection ... Nothing appears less likely than an insurrection, but nothing is more necessary."[14]

It is the spontaneity of the Occupy movement that has been both its most powerful tactic (keeping the State, media, and "the public" on edge and off guard) as well as its most internally divisive characteristic. Lefebvre notes that spontaneity can lead to "dis-alienation through unfettered speech, street activities, and spontaneous disorder"[15] – the disruption of everyday life – "what is really involved is action and an activist movement endowed with intense, rapid, and lucid perception of immediate possibilities."[16]

The Invisible Committee, just a few years before the occupations broke out, similarly celebrate open and spontaneous structure – and seem to anticipate the Occupy movement: "No leader, no demands, no organization, but words, gestures, complicities ... An insurrectionary surge may be nothing more than a multiplication of communes, their coming into contact and forming ties."[17]

The Occupy movement has seen the realization of just these structures and strategies that allow for, and in fact depend upon, horizontal spontaneity. *Unfettered speech*: in general assemblies and at the constant open mic soapboxes. *Dis-alienation*: I cannot count the times I have seen in people's faces, heard in their voices, the sense of having found a venue, a means, a community to express their outrage and hope, a space in which they can become engaged, politically relevant, empowered. The constant presence of *insurrectionary possibility*: repeatedly, in the early weeks at Occupy Vancouver – as elsewhere across the global movement – a street march, a rally, the occupation of some particular civic or commercial space, happened instantly as someone or some small group walked through the camp shouting, "Mic check" and called for the particular action, which people could choose to join or not.[18]

The criticism of spontaneity – which is also the criticism of "violence" (see below) and confrontational tactics generally – is that although it can be "dis-alienating" for the participants in the spontaneous action (who suddenly find themselves working as a cohesive collective body that can actually *do something*), it can at the same time be alienating for those watching from the sidelines and trying to decide whether they are "in or out." Inevitably, we are led toward discussions of a "diversity of tactics"; spontaneity, however, is hardly a "tactic" (if it is truly spontaneous). Indignation must be respected and given room – it is what impels us, spontaneously, to take to the streets to challenge power, privilege, and authority. But it will only – on its own – take us so far. Spontaneity doesn't really *think* – but it can forge a space within which thought (and discussion and learning) can occur. And that is worth the price of entry.

There is no point in romanticizing spontaneity (or process, for that matter, as I discuss below). The need now, as the Occupy movement strides forward, is to direct this spontaneity into longevity – to fashion a movement that will carry on its work for years to come; if it is all and only about spontaneity (which 1968 seems largely to be in hindsight) then we will be over and done with before we realize that we have even begun.

ON PROCESS

Much has been made already of the focus on "process" in the Occupy movement. This, like spontaneity, has thrilled many participants, empowering and dis-alienating them, but it has also frustrated those wanting to speed social change along, streamline the decision-making process to respond quickly to volatile situations, and, at times, just *get shit done*.

Lefebvre notes a situation that has become even worse today: "People have lost the habit of participation and decision-making, except where consumers' goods are concerned."[19] So there is pedagogical social value in the movement's focus on process: we need, desperately, to relearn the habits of social participation, community building, collective responsibility, and decision making, as they have generally been marginalized if not outright eradicated in consumer society. And there is – despite its sometimes slow, sometimes awkward and frustrating inertia – power in the horizontal, "leaderless," decentralized process being worked out in the occupations around the world.

"The striking characteristic of the movement," Lefebvre writes, as though once again addressing the situation we now face, "is that it was able to hold its own without apparatus or institution, that it had an organization without fixed structure, and that it took politically intelligent decisions without a pre-established program and 'leaders' (there were only spokesmen)."[20]

In 2011, most occupations managed to pass founding documents and statements of some kind – many of them stirring, galvanizing expressions of social outrage and renewed social commitment. Most occupations internally organized their encampments; provided food, shelter, and medical attention to their constituents; and set up libraries and educational programs, speaker series, and discussion groups. Most occupations organized protests, marches, and direct actions, liaising with the media and producing their own media releases, documentation, and cultural records. Most occupations managed to hold their own against weeks of pressure from the aggressive machinery of the State – a hostile media, a litigious government, and a belligerent police force – not to mention an increasingly dubious and caustic (and highly manufactured, through disinformation) "public opinion." All this – "without apparatus or institution" – but with process.

Nevertheless, not everything about the focus on process is ideal. The Invisible Committee – again anticipating the occupations – cautions that the "business of voting and deciding a winner is enough to turn the assembly into a nightmare, into a theatre where all the various pretenders to power confront each other … An assembly is not a place for decisions but for *talk*, for free speech exercised without a goal."[21] The point here is that smaller, semi-autonomous affinity groups are often better decision-making mechanisms than large general assemblies, which are ideal fora for discussion of the broadest issues, checking the movement's temperature, and for generating ideas and the broad outlines of plans, but are prone to getting bogged down in their own processes, to polarization, divisions, grandstanding, and being hijacked (or at least endlessly delayed) by individuals or small splinter groups (some of whom may be *agents provocateurs*) that may have anything but decision making and "getting shit done" on their minds. Many occupations have brought in "spokes-council" models for just these reasons, freeing their general assemblies up to be discussion fora and "think tanks" for group intelligence. "There is no need to choose between the fetishism of spontaneity and organizational control," the Invisible Committee opines.[22] They can interact, dialectically.

True democracies always face this process dilemma: how to mediate between inclusivity and decision making, openness and end results. The larger the group, the more difficult this process becomes. Process, to remain free and open, paradoxically requires a great deal of internal structure and organization – ideally along horizontal, decentralized, rotating, and federated lines. The "process" that is so much the substance of the Occupy movement is still, almost everywhere, a work in progress. But this is crucial work, the most difficult work – in part because it engages the very opposite of spontaneity and indignation – and because it truly is the imaginative creation of a new social formation.

ON VIOLENCE

Lefebvre links spontaneity with violence, the street with conflict. The first thing to say about violence and the Occupy movement is that virtually all the actual violence associated with the movement has been perpetrated by the police as they have attempted to intimidate and remove encampments, with occupiers being remarkably consistent in their commitment to non-violence as a tactic. The second thing to say about violence and social movements generally is that we need to seriously revisit our definition of "violence" – a word that the media, and even many activists, are currently abusing.

Although the arguments can be complicated, we cannot define property destruction in the same terms as causing direct bodily harm, which is exactly what happens around discussions of direct-action tactics. Violence is doing physical or psychological harm to a living being; it is dependent upon there being a living organism capable of receiving and experiencing the violent act. To conflate property destruction with violence is to bestow personhood on private property (as the United States has done in attributing legal personhood to corporations). This is only defensible under a system where the accumulation of capital, based on the private ownership of property, is the *sine qua non* of "the common good."

While media and government representatives – the defenders of private property rights and capital accumulation – decry vandalism as the most wanton of crimes, "the US [and Canadian!] media is simply constitutionally incapable of reporting acts of police repression as 'violence,'" as David Graeber notes.[23] The association of protest with "violence" is a means of containing and suppressing dissent, as well as an excuse to remove some of our democratic rights (which inescapably and by definition involve some "confrontational" situations). It is a containment strategy launched by the State, through the corporate media. This is what is at work each time there is a reference to "violent protestors." Hegemony is being reasserted.

The Occupy movement comes up against the problematic definitions of "violence" because it is constituted as a critique of and direct action against the system of capital accumulation based on the private and unequal ownership of property. That is, the Occupy movement – not unlike other social movements of the past – is attempting to redefine "the common good" in the midst of broad social and economic crises. Part of this active redefinition may involve symbolic and material challenges to the edifice and structures of the capitalist system. It will also involve contravening and contesting laws that exist merely to protect private property and accumulation rights – something that becomes a moral imperative amid extreme social inequalities and in the face of a dire ecological crisis brought on by these very capitalist structures.

Within Occupy Vancouver, as elsewhere in the global movement, debates have raged about tactics, with many people raising the concern that certain militant or so-called violent tactics will alienate large segments of the movement's potential supporters. This is based upon a misunderstanding of both the tactics (and their supposed violence) in question and the relation of the movement to "the public."

To briefly address the latter before returning to the question of violence, the Occupy movement has often seemed driven by a representational logic by which the movement's acts and statements should somehow seem to "represent" the entire 99%. This is both absurdly impossible and socially undesirable, a sort of "lowest common denominator" strategy that can only lead to a completely ineffectual mirroring of the status quo. But the Occupy movement actually embodies a different sort of politics than the representational game of "winning a majority." It is about direct participatory democracy. The 99% is not a campaign platform, and not a projected vote tally. It is a recognition of renewed and extreme class conflict, as well as a recognition that the vast majority of people do not presently, but certainly can (by stepping forward to participate in a movement for social change) exercise social power. It is not a matter of convincing people to "join" the 99%, but rather, to realize that they *are* the 99%, and so to act in their own collective best interests.

Much of the concern about supposedly alienating militancy has coalesced around Black Bloc tactics, perhaps given no clearer expression than in award-winning journalist Chris Hedges's (one of the Occupy movement's leading supporters) condemnation of the Bloc as a "cancer" in the movement.[24] The focus here is squarely on the idea that the Bloc is an embodiment of violence and that such violence will alienate the 99% and thus weaken the movement. Zakk Flash is among a host of anarchist and movement thinkers who have stepped up to critique this position, accusing Hedges of having "bought into the American Empire's fallacy that direct action and organization in our communities is unfavorable and that submission to elected authorities is the only way to enact permanent change."[25]

David Graeber has also been an eloquent defender of Black Bloc tactics (which, he correctly emphasizes, are *tactics*, not "groups" or "organizations," as Hedges seems to suggest), particularly in terms of how they are situated within the debate about employing a "diversity of tactics."[26] Graeber defines Black Bloc tactics (in which militant activists dress in black clothes, wear masks, sometimes confront police, and, occasionally, carry out acts of corporate property destruction) as "a gesture of anonymity, solidarity, and to indicate to others that they are prepared, if the situation calls for it, for militant action … One of the ideas of having a Black Bloc is that everyone who comes to a protest should know where the people likely to engage in militant action are, and thus easily be able to avoid it if that's what they wish to do."[27] Thus in this reading of Black Bloc tactics, it's a matter of setting clear boundaries, as well as a matter of sending a clear signal to those both participating in and opposing a particular action: the stakes are high, and we are willing to take risks to achieve this movement's goals.

A diversity of tactics, Graeber continues, "means leaving such matters up to individual conscience, rather than imposing a code on anyone. Partly, this is because imposing such a code invariably backfires."

Occupy Vancouver has indeed experienced just the sort of problems of "policing peace" that Graeber describes in his response to Hedges. In this way, mandating non-violence itself becomes a form of violence as those who are unwilling to completely swear off a diversity of tactics are subjected to relentless personal harassment and bullying. What occupiers need to realize is that too narrow a definition of "violence" buys into the logic of the system they are trying to oppose and unnecessarily hamstrings activists (in many cases disallowing the civil disobedience that lies at the heart of resistance movements). It's also important to understand that no one tactic works at all times and in all places.

The reality is, if this moment is to be any different – if it is actually going to *change* anything this time – it can't rely on finding the perfect tactic from the past, nor can it hope to latch on to a new, as yet unimagined tactic for the twenty-first century. What it needs to do is flexibly employ a variety of tactics as opportunity presents itself and context determines. These often contradictory tactics, given room for full expression, allow the movement to remain open to the participation of a diverse range of groups and interests and keeps an ever more pervasive police state off balance.

We also need to question the logic that supposes that the "wrong tactics" will alienate potential supporters. Our governments engage in acts of violence on a regular basis. We call it "policing" or, in its more extreme forms, "war." Unfortunately, we witness or experience violence in our societies on a daily basis, whether it is an assault in the street, racist or sexist language, systematic marginalization of immigrant groups, a bloody video game, a hockey game, or a hockey riot. Society absorbs these acts and images and moves on. While I am not suggesting that we should accept violence as "normal," I think we should ask ourselves why we are so convinced that any activist "violence" (by which we typically mean that property is purposely or even symbolically damaged) will immediately alienate the "general public" and condemn our movement to the dustbin of criminal history. Why have we allowed many forms of civil disobedience to be labeled as "violent," "criminal," and beyond the pale? (It is worth noting that this is clearly not the case in much of the rest of the world, where confrontational protests do not alienate the "general public" – many of whom, we should also remember, are right there protesting in the street.)

Just as "the most common way people give up their power is by thinking they don't have any,"[28] the most common way social movements are defeated is by thinking they don't have any tactical choices. Voting? That's out – doesn't work. Armed revolution? No way – the State is too well armed and organized. Besides, we simply become the system we're trying to replace. Lobbying and NGOs? Too tame, ineffective, complicit, part of the system. Marches, occupations, demonstrations? Maybe – but a little predictable. The police are well trained for dealing with those. Targeted property destruction, monkey wrenching, rioting in the streets? Too alienating. Too aggressive. Too easily dismissed.

By way of concluding this discussion, I turn to the example of the civil rights movement, where divergent tactics jostled together throughout the late 1950s and the 1960s. Herbert Haines, in *Black Radicals and the Civil Rights Mainstream*, argues that the diversity of activist formations in the civil rights movement – from Martin Luther King's Southern Baptists organizing marches to the Black Panthers' more militant and confrontational actions – actually added to its effectiveness, counter to arguments which might suggest that "protest groups must refrain from tactics and statements which would alienate prospective supporters."[29] Indeed, Haines finds that "the turmoil which the militants created was indispensible to black progress, and indeed, black radicalization had the net effect of enhancing the bargaining position of mainstream civil rights groups and hastening the attainment of many of their goals."[30]

The Occupy movement would be well advised to keep this example in mind when it comes up against the problem of enforced non-violence. As Haines notes, "since ideological and tactical unanimity are so exceptional as to be virtually nonexistent," the only real option for viable social movements is a "strategic balance" which must and indeed "can be struck, a symbiosis between radicals and moderates. In this relationship radicals specialize in generating crises which elites must deal with, while moderates specialize in offering relatively unthreatening avenues of escape."[31]

As many activists have noted – even supporters of a diversity of tactics – non-violence is the right tactic for this movement, in this historical moment. What is uncertain is what we will define as "violent," and what we will allow under the category of "non-violence." What is also yet to be determined is whether – contra Hannah Arendt – a revolution can take place outside the domain of violence.[32] As each non-violent move is met by increasing police violence (real violence, causing harm to individuals) and the piecemeal outlawing of the majority of non-violent tactics, we will have to see what tactics are left.

ON AUTONOMY

There were a number of turning points for Occupy Vancouver, many of which highlighted the tensions in the movement between its "radicals" and "moderates." Such tensions were clear from the outset, when some early organizers sought permission to set up a cooperative relationship with the City of Vancouver and the Vancouver Police Department (though they failed to adequately seek such permission from and cooperation with local First Nations). During the encampment (October 15 to November 21, 2011) there were more or less daily disagreements about militant action: either the movement was being too militant to engage the 99% or it was not being militant enough to be taken seriously as a force for social change.

Moments that stand out (and which I discuss in more detail in relevant "dispatches" in part two) include the overdoses, the lighting of the sacred fire, and of course the eviction itself. However, I want to focus for now on the "declaration of autonomy" made by the Tent City Council on November 4.[33] Tent City Council member Kiki read the declaration at a press conference held on the Vancouver Art Gallery steps. I include here the complete declaration as transcribed by and reproduced in the *Vancouver Courier*:

> We want to make this clear that this is a message [from] the people of tent city and it's been consensed upon within tent city council. It has not been brought to the GA [general assembly]. This is a message specifically from the tenters to the people of Vancouver and the movement as a whole.
>
> We want to start off by recognizing that Occupy Vancouver tent city is located on unceded Coast Salish territory. Furthermore we declare our encampment to be an autonomous state ruled directly by those who live in it as part of the global Occupy movement.
>
> It was consensed [sic] upon last night in the GA that all orders or threats from various municipal or provincial agencies will only be addressed if brought to the GA through proper protocol.
>
> We want to go further to make it clear that orders brought to us or to the GA from outside agencies will be considered only in an advisory capacity. The members of tent council have consensed this is a self-ruling autonomous zone and while we do welcome informed advice from relevant authorities, the ultimate decision-making authority rests in the hands of the people.
>
> We are ruling ourselves peacefully here and we will continue to do so.
>
> Within our zones we are creating a fully functioning committee that directly serves the needs and the interests of the people. Our goal here is to provide the social services needed to sustain a healthy and vibrant community. It is imperative to do so, not only in order to support the Occupy movement, but also to deliver basic social services that are not being met by the current system to the people of Vancouver. This includes basic needs such

as shelter, food and medical care. [The intent here at tent city is] to cover education. We've got childcare [we're] working on [and] other modes of healing that are not accessible to people without the money to get them.

We want to make it clear we will provide these services for free to all and that we will continue to expand our operations-to build from the ground up parallel systems outside the zone so we may be completely autonomous.

We are proving our ability to provide for ourselves each day that our community peacefully grows. We welcome all the individuals who make up the 99 per cent to contribute to the success of the community by volunteering their relevant skills and training.

We want to make it clear that you do not have to be a tenter to support tent city, Every service needed in the City of Vancouver is also needed in here as well. We urge you to join us in whichever way you can.

It has been consensed upon within tent council that weapons are not welcome within these grounds, nor are those who carry them.

It has also been consensed upon that while we appreciate the city's concern for our health and safety and look forward to maintaining friendly relations with the city workers, fire department, municipal authorities and the police, the authority of these individuals and their agencies is not recognized in the autonomous zone.

As such, those working for those agencies are still welcome to join the movement as sovereign individuals and assist the movement by applying their skills and training here to meet the needs of the movement. However, we want to make it clear as an autonomous zone, as an encampment on unceded native land, their institutional authority is not recognized here.

We govern ourselves. We also want to make it clear should the police choose not to respect our decisions, we are willing to stand in the way of these weapons in order to protect our autonomy. [applause interrupted transcript recording]

We would like to reiterate that this is not a dispute with the city, but rather an ongoing battle.

For the mainstream media, and indeed for a number of occupiers, this spelled the beginning of the end. Anarchist philosophy – always present, if not always named, in most of the movement's basic processes and practices – was now laid bare on the encampment's surface. And there were many who were not happy with this "coming-out party."

Whatever else we might say about this document, it is certainly the most militant statement to come out of Occupy Vancouver. One might question it on pragmatic grounds. (How "autonomous" would the camp likely be from a city increasingly bringing its State apparatuses to bear on the small downtown occupation?) But it is important to remember that the statement was made *between the two overdoses* that so rocked the occupation and frenzied the media – the first, on November 3, and the second, fatal overdose, on November 5.[34] It also occurred in the midst of, and in response to, increasing pressure from the City, via its fire department, for the encampment to comply with fire safety regulations or face eviction.

The City's expressed concern about fire safety was patently ridiculous and merely an excuse for officials to order the removal of the encampment.[35] It would have been easy at this point for Occupy Vancouver to have caved in altogether, packed up and left the Vancouver Art Gallery lawns – especially as the media (and "public opinion" in its wake) turned all the more aggressively against the occupation. The Tent City Council declaration of autonomy let the City and the media know that militant elements in the movement would not be so easily removed. It also affirmed the encampment's intention and commitment – even amid the difficulties of State pressure, a media circus, and even death – to handling its own affairs and building an alternate society separate from (though inescapably occupying the same space as) the crumbling shell of the existing system. Some scoffed at such an idea, and took the overdose death as a clear example of the encampment's *inability* to "take care of itself." However, overdose deaths sadly occur with alarming regularity in Vancouver; if Occupy Vancouver could not save someone's life, neither can the City of Vancouver, as is evident on a weekly basis. But as the first overdose victim who *was* saved indicates, Occupy Vancouver was in some circumstances very much able to "save" its own constituents, and certainly paid closer attention to its marginal members than the City does. The Tent City declaration called the bluff of both the City of Vancouver *and* the more reformist elements in Occupy Vancouver.

The declaration of autonomy and its aftermath also revealed (and in fact directly addressed) something else: a growing division between Tent City and the GA, mirrored in the division between the "doers" and the "process junkies." Increasingly, "anarchist" became something of a derogatory term in the camp, and the "peace police" either upped their campaign to rout out and exclude all potential "violence" (peddling the most ambiguous and self-defeating definition of the term), or left the movement altogether.

Direct action, when properly theorized, is in fact the combination of thought and action, process and presentation. There is no real division between thinking and doing, process and presentation, when one fully engages direct action as both philosophy and praxis. Occupy Vancouver had all the elements of a vital social movement in place (a commitment to a non-violent, inclusive, and consensus-based social process, *and* an urgent militancy ready to spontaneously defy authority and enter the streets to perform direct actions), but it has yet to find a way of working with the dialectical energies it has thus set in motion, rather than letting them tear the movement apart.

Occupy Vancouver's inability to adequately articulate its driving dialectic led to other related problems as well. The meaning of "inclusivity" has been much disputed, and abused, as people have continually been confused by the relation of inclusivity to the establishment of proper, safe, interpersonal boundaries (this has especially been a problem when it comes to gender relations).[36] Those wanting as lax and open a definition of "inclusivity" as possible decry the actions of others – once again, the so-called "process junkies" – who are concerned to establish interpersonal boundaries and clear codes of conduct. The same arguments have spilled over into accusations that those wanting to raise issues of gender, race, and ability are "derailing" the movement from its core economic message – an absurd position as clearly none of these issues can reasonably be separated, and the structure of the whole crisis is manifest in each of its parts.

Some of this divisiveness has in fact led to splits in the movement, as groups wanting to more or less formally ban all illegal action – groups rejecting anarchism (though seemingly unaware of their philosophical position or how embedded their practices and ideas are in the movement) or groups decrying discussions of feminism and other issues as "divisive" or "marginal" – have seceded from the main movement, or worse, driven women and other activists away from the often corrosive atmosphere that was allowed to develop around the movement. Paradoxically, these same people who decry "violence" and "crime" as giving the movement a bad name (thus supposedly alienating the 99%) also accuse the anarchists of being too bogged down in process to actually *do* anything (or, alternatively, capable only of "meaningless violence").

As of the spring of 2012, Occupy Vancouver has more or less devolved into autonomous affinity groups, many of which are doing excellent, productive work on a variety of fronts, and most of which reunite for larger actions that touch the core of the movement: economic injustice, environmental exploitation, and political corruption. Kiki's declaration rings true in the end: Occupy Vancouver continues to exercise its autonomy, and is – structurally and in other ways, too – even more consciously "anarchist" than it was in the fall of 2011.[37]

ON REFORM VERSUS REVOLUTION

What I am tracing here takes the form of an unresolved tension, a dialectical tug-of-war between two seemingly irreconcilable currents in the forming and already transforming Occupy movement –

perhaps in all social movements. Spontaneity versus planning, militant direct action versus passive, non-violent resistance, are just some of its formations. What perhaps lies beneath these various tensions is the old struggle between reform and revolution, that dialectic that has driven all social activism over the course of the history of the left. The Occupy movement's unfolding indicates that this old either/or logic might now be in the process of being replaced by a more dynamic both/and formation. Again, Lefebvre and May 1968 point the direction in which the Occupy movement has evolved: "It tried in particular to free itself from an old dilemma – either all-embracing, total revolution, or fragmented activities that must inevitably degenerate into reformism."[38] Such "alternatives," Levebvre goes on, "that at one time seemed relevant options and dilemmas appear obsolete today."[39]

Although Lefebvre suggests here that the old paradigms were exhausted, it seems that in 1968 we were not quite ready to be done with the reform versus revolution argument. Fingers began pointing once again as May 1968 faded into the neoliberal haze, resulting at best in minor reforms. As the decades wore on, the neoliberal moment perhaps had its nadir, though not yet the full implementation of its program, whose effects we are still feeling, in the early 1990s with the fall of the Soviet Union, Francis Fukuyama's declaration that "history" (that history of class struggle, as well as the struggle between reform and revolution) had come to its "end," and the ascendency of Margaret Thatcher's proclamation that there was "no alternative" to the free market and the "democratic" electoral system overseen by the doctrines of unfettered economic growth. Indeed, Thatcher spoke for most neoliberals when she declared that there was "no such thing as society," thereby ending any debates about social change (how could anything change – whether by reformist or revolutionary programs – if it didn't even exist?).

The anti-globalization movement(s) of the late 1990s and early 2000s were a clear sign that all was not said and done – a seemingly brief window when revolutionary and activist tactics stormed back onto the re-emerging scene of struggle before being buried (or obscured – in North America at least) once again under the "war on terror" and its smokescreen for renegade economic excess. It is in this light that I would like to turn to two able guides,

Richard Day and David Graeber, for their insights about this moment and especially for their speculations about the potential for future forms of resistance. Day's and Graeber's musings on future modalities of resistance, written in the years just before the 2008 financial crash and its aftermath, in many ways anticipated the arrival of the Occupy movement.

For Day, the new social movements that emerged under the banner of anti-globalization reach back to the spirit of May 1968 (as, I argue, they also gesture forward to the occupations of 2011). In doing so, they reach beyond the binary of reform versus revolution (recall Levebvre's assessment above) into what Day describes, in *Gramsci is Dead*, as a post-hegemonic space.

Day begins by noting the ideological terrain upon which, in hindsight, the anti-globalization movement was an instructive but temporary intrusion: "Neoliberal entrepreneurs, intellectuals and journalists have been working to reverse the flow of social change, and they have been largely successful in doing so," seeking – and achieving – hegemony on a vast scale.[40] In this context,

> the obvious answer is to try to establish a counter-hegemony, to shift the historical balance back, as much as possible, in favour of the oppressed ... To argue in this way, however, is to remain within the logic of neoliberalism; it is to accept what I call the *hegemony of hegemony* ... What is most interesting about contemporary activism is that some groups are breaking out of this trap by operating *non*-hegemonically rather than *counter*-hegemonically. They seek radical change, but not through taking or influencing state power, and in so doing they challenge the logic of hegemony at its very core.[41]

From a non-hegemonic perspective, there is neither a center to be reformed nor an opposing power to be overturned by revolution. There are simply relations to be forged, communities to be built, and a commons to be held in trust by its commoners. Power is neither to be tempered nor seized; it is to be vacated. Thus the point of a social movement is not (at least not limited to) opposition, critique, or challenges to authority, but is really about imagining and building alternatives.

This sheds light on a number of aspects of the Occupy movement that have perplexed observers – and sometimes even participants. The non-hegemonic impulse is, for one thing, related to the question of demands, or rather, the absence of a list of specific demands coming out of the movement. Day refers to a "*politics of demand*": "This mode of social action assumes the existence of a dominant nation attached to a monopolistic State, which must be persuaded to give the gifts of *recognition* and *integration* to subordinate identities and communities" – to which he opposes a "*politics of the act*."[42] Again, we can trace the line that runs from May 1968, through the anti-globalization protests, and into the formal logic of the Occupy movement, which has been, if nothing else, a thoroughgoing *politics of the act*, sidestepping the blatantly ineffectual established political channels to set up its own model society within the crumbling shell of disaster capitalism. This through line might best be described as a re-emergence of anarchist tactics, anarchist strategies, and an anarchist vision of a Stateless society – direct, participatory democracy, consensus-based decision making, and a constituent-based politics.

Day's analysis directs our attention to thus another aspect of the perplexing modalities of the Occupy movement: its "leader-less," horizontal, and networked structure. To appoint or recognize leaders, like acknowledging a State to which demands can be put, is to perpetuate the hierarchical, unequal, and exploitative system the Occupy movement is attempting to displace. It's an old idea about means and ends: if you want a free, equal, and open society, you have to use free, equal, and open means to achieve it. The trouble is, such means often seem unequal to the task of changing, let alone defeating, the highly centralized and militarized system that currently exists.

Such an impression misses the tactical point of a *politics of the act*: one isn't *merely* trying to change or defeat what already exists (at least, not primarily, not exclusively); one is, more importantly, trying to create *new* social relations, a *new* society, something *entirely other than* what we are currently saddled with. What characterizes the movements from May 1968 through anti-globalization and into Occupy is their creative and imaginative experimenting with alternative social formations, as well as their unwillingness to simply engage in the winner-take-all struggle for hegemonic control embodied in reformist election platforms *and* revolutionary takeovers. Day refers to this as

> the radical impulse of post-1968 French theory – the impulse to create alternatives to the state and corporate forms rather than just work within them … by articulating how a non-reformist and non-revolutionary politics can in fact lead to progressive social change that responds to the needs of disparate identities without attempting to subsume them under a common project.[43]

David Graeber – my other guide to the anti-globalization movement and its continuities with the Occupy movement – traces the outlines of this same "radical impulse" to the question of tactics:

> Where once it seemed that the only alternatives to marching along with signs were either Gandhian non-violent civil disobedience or outright insurrection, groups like the Direct Action Network, Reclaim the Streets, Black Blocs or Tute Bianche have all, in their own ways, been trying to map out a completely new territory in between.[44]

In *Direct Action*, his "ethnography" of the 2001 demonstrations at the Quebec City Summit of the Americas, Graeber further outlines this "territory in between" by essentially arguing for a "situation of permanent revolution" through which "freedom becomes the struggle itself."[45] Rejecting both reformist programs ("one does not solicit the state … one proceeds as if the state does not exist") and "the old assumption that a single uprising or successful civil war could, as it were, neutralize the entire apparatus of structural violence," Graeber looks to the "quality" of the "insurrectionary moment" repeatedly unfolding via frequent direct actions and collective participation in the redrawing of daily life.[46] This "quality" – one which I know many occupiers here in Vancouver and around the world have viscerally experienced – is characterized by "the effect of throwing horizons of possibility wide open," "unleash[ing] the human imagination," and enabling "a vast outpouring of improvisation."[47] This is the creativity of insurrection, the enabling and catalyzing excitement it brings, the sense it instills that another world is indeed possible, and that there is no way to resist an idea whose time has come. It is a "quality" experienced outside of both rational and emotional decisions about whether one is "reformist" or "revolutionary."

I agree with Graeber's assessment that most people never "seriously considered the possibility that they might trigger the Revolution in the traditional messianic sense"; instead, what we find in the permanent revolution of direct action campaigns (and occupations) is a *process* by which we learn to imagine and live in the new world we are ushering into being via a series of "foretastes" and "experiences of visionary inspiration" as "the painstaking effort to create alternatives" unfolds.[48]

We are still in the midst of the anti-globalization (or social justice) movement – it has simply shifted its name and tactics slightly as its successes have brought more people into the fold. We are still in the moment opened by May 1968 – the moment of spontaneous possibility that arises as we spill into the streets to demand system-wide change now and at once, as we declare ourselves to be unwilling to do the work of the 1% for one more day, as we step outside of the existing system, as though shedding ourselves of some old, restrictive clothes.

But of course, we aren't really outside of anything. It's not possible to ever be fully outside of something as systemic, as pervasive, as global capitalism. But we've found that we can puncture it and gaze beyond. And we've found that there are others noticing this tear in the fabric of the real, who are also looking outside, and who are noticing one another. And we've begun to imagine something else, something different, and to experiment with its forms and processes – right there in the breach we have made in the real.

Recasting Day and Graeber's arguments slightly, I would suggest that now we need to simultaneously pursue reform *and* revolution – the amelioration of the current system *and* the replacement of the current system. The problem we face in the reform versus revolution debate is that reform is too slow, and revolution seems too fast and too absolute, too total and all at once. Employing a "diversity of strategies" just as we would a "diversity of tactics," we can and I think must pursue, simultaneously, agitation for reforms (opposition to specific programs, bills, and legislation which, in the current situation, often means militating against austerity measures) as well as the imagination, construction, and experimental implementation of a radically alternative new revolutionary society that operates outside of, and in confident opposition to, the existing system. These seem to be, but in fact are not, mutually exclusive or contradictory. They describe an invigorating tension that drives social movements forward. We begin at once with the realization of the new world we want, and with the amelioration of the ailing old world we reject. We accept that while we *build the new world within the shell of the old*, there are many who need immediate help and relief as parts of that crumbling shell fall upon them, or who suffer from their exclusion from the crumbling structure of the old system – relief that comes possibly quickest (if only partially) through existing channels. What we enact in our direct, participatory actions is both a reformation and a revolution – a new construction that at once "fixes" and "replaces" that which is.

ON THE RE-EMERGENCE OF CLASS STRUGGLE

In the occupations of 2011, in North America at least, there was little sense of "blocks" of students and workers, so identified, coming together. The occupiers were, however, "workers" and "students," by and large. A distinctly new unity was in play – the 99%, a renewed sense of "the public" occupying "public space," all of us who, whatever our social and cultural position, work in order to maintain the extreme wealth of an infinitesimally small contingent of the citizenry.[49] Meanwhile, the economic and ecological systems around us crumble and degrade.

Day, examining the anti-globalization movement, writes about the nebulous struggle where "*there is no single enemy* against which the newest social movements are fighting."[50] The difference, now, some ten years after the height of the anti-globalization movement, is that we are beginning to narrow down the question of the "enemy" (the 1%) and their "location" ("Wall Street" – though there are obviously other important locations throughout the capitalist network). This is increasingly described as an awakening, as a well-known sign from Occupy Wall Street declares: "Dear 1%. We Were Asleep. Now We've Woken Up. Signed, the 99%." The statement "We are the 99%," chanted at rallies and reproduced on websites collecting stories of contemporary economic difficulty, "politicizes a statistic that expresses capitalism's reliance on fundamental inequality … this 'we' is a class, one of two opposed and hostile classes, those who have and control wealth, and those who do not," as Jodi Dean writes in *Occupy! Scenes from Occupied America*.[51]

Class consciousness – the awareness that there are stark inequalities, and that one belongs to a broad collective with common social circumstances and common social goals – can be a driving force for social change. It's also one that has been largely missing from political debate in the developed world for many decades now – even in May 1968 and later in the anti-globalization movement it took a backseat to burgeoning "cultural" and geo-political awakenings. Part of what a renewed focus on class brings to the table – aside from a focus on broad political-economic structures and systemic biases – is a sense of motivating companionship in a shared struggle. We see this in the overwhelmingly positive, even optimistic character of the movement: "This isn't the kind of world we want to live in, and it's we who have to decide what world we do want. We know we can change it, and we're having a great time going about it."[52] That "we" is a class – possibly the largest and most diverse class in history – discovering its strength and potential.

The point here is not to resurrect some old idea of the inevitable, teleological course of history. There is nothing inevitable about the triumph of the working class – history has made that clear. What the Occupy movement has done is returned to us a language in which class conflict and extreme inequality – always present under capitalism – is once again noticeable, expressible, and available to critique. This can only strengthen the position of those of us who are struggling to change the present course of history. It is also, in Slavoj Žižec's analogy, a way of giving us back our "red ink."

In his October 2011 speech at Occupy Wall Street, Žižec tells "an old joke from communist times." Someone banished to Siberia, knowing the censors would read his mail, establishes a code with his correspondents: blue ink will be for falsehoods that appease the censors, red ink for the truth. His first letter from Siberia is entirely in blue ink, and sings the praises of the life of exile. Its final sentence notes that the only thing he is missing is red ink. "This is how we live," Žižec notes; "we have all the freedoms we want. But what we are missing is red ink: the language to articulate our non-freedom … this is what you are doing here," he tells the occupiers. "You are giving all of us red ink."[53]

To provide red ink is to provide a language for critique – a language of renewed class conflict ("We are the 99%"). It is also to supply a language in which new alternatives to the "there is no alternative" capitalist system can be envisioned and experimented with. The entire Occupy movement is written in red ink, and we are only just beginning to be able to read what is written there.

3.

> Revolutionary movements do not spread by
> contamination but by resonance … An
> insurrection is not like a plague or a forest
> fire – a linear process which spreads from
> place to place after an initial spark. It rather
> takes the shape of a music, whose focal
> points, though dispersed in time and space,
> succeed in imposing the rhythm of their own
> vibrations, always taking on more density.
>
> – THE INVISIBLE COMMITTEE
> *The Coming Insurrection*

Whenever revolutionary activity has spread beyond the bounds
of a single country – whenever it seems to have leaped from one
country to another, threatening world revolution – it has done so
by rhythm and resonance. This was the case in Europe in 1848
(when the songs, language, and ideas of the French Revolution
once again made their rounds) and again in Eastern Europe in
1989; it was also the case in the Arab Spring of early 2011 and in
the *Indignado* and Occupy movements later that year. Rhythms of
this sort "impose" themselves via repetition – but they become
interesting, affective rhythms because of their subtle variations. A
new pattern is set and the people engage with it, repeating it and
varying it day by day (take, for example, what unfolded over
several weeks in Tahrir Square: a broad cross-section of society,
dropping out of their normal routines to stand together, all day,
day after day, until real change is realized). Another people
observe something in that new pattern – see its similarities to and

differences from past patterns. As the people realize the adaptability of the new pattern, it begins to move with the rhythm, repeating and varying the music. (In this manner, taking the square, calling for wholesale change moves from Egypt to Spain's Puerta del Sol.) Once again, as the pattern establishes itself uniquely among that people, it strikes up another new resonance with still another people, who once again repeat and vary the rhythm. (It is September and Wall Street is occupied.)

Strangely, the old pattern of behavior – the one in which we swing and stagger between hope and despair, disaster and distraction, fear and consumption – is also a rhythm, a resonance we become used to – like addicts, or like abused children whose horrors are part of their "normal." To shift rhythms, to replace an older, ailing rhythm with a newer, more vital one, we have to keep hearing the new resonance, and we have to keep dancing to it – even when it seems foolish to do so, even when we feel alone and vulnerable. On October 15, 2011, I marched through Vancouver's streets with five thousand people. During a march in February 2012, I was one of twenty people. Was it a little embarrassing to be so exposed? Yes. But we kept marching. Did it indicate that the revolutionary moment was over? No. There were marches in other cities, all over the world, at the same time. And every week here in Vancouver there are marches and demonstrations and actions of some kind. We keep marching. We are establishing a new rhythm. We are getting used to it. It will take time.

Social media is one way the new rhythm is being established. I do not hail the Internet in utopian terms. The reality of organizing social movements online is fraught with problems. It is very good for setting a time and place for something to happen, and for letting people know what is happening; it is not very good for discussion or working through the finer ideological or tactical points. One remarkable thing about the current wave of revolutionary activity is that it is *both* (and simultaneously) a new virtual practice carried out through social media and *still*, necessarily, a very old practice that depends upon actual bodies occupying actual physical spaces in very material cities. Both of these, entwined, at once.

But social media is without question one way that the new social rhythms are being taken up quickly and passed from individual to individual, community to community – regardless of where they might be in the world. The fact that the corporate State has been so keyed into the phenomenon (the SOPA bill in the US and Bill C-30 in Canada) is enough to indicate that the Internet is indeed one of the new battlegrounds where bottom-up distributed systems clash with top-down attempts to legislate control.[54] This struggle is the mirror image of the struggle in the streets where States are also enacting new legislation to directly suppress dissent (the NDAA in the US and Bill C-78 in Quebec).[55] This is, ultimately, an extension of the renewed class conflict. As the Zapatistas declared in the mid-1990s, "We are the network, all of us who resist."[56] What is being worked out now in the Occupy movement is how to "network" our activities online *and* in the street, as we must continue to be, stridently and consistently, *against* everywhere and anywhere.

★

What we need now is a different "shock doctrine," a different sense of the "opportunity" offered by "crisis."[57] This would be an opportunity not, as in the case of capitalist opportunism, for privatization and a further curtailing of the commons, but for a remaking of the public sphere, a return to the commons, in the spirit of bringing healing to the earth and human society. This is the agenda of the Occupy movement: a renewed recognition of, demand for, and defense of the commons. The economy cannot simply be given a green veneer. We know this will not be enough. "We have to see that the economy is not 'in' crisis, the economy is itself the crisis," the Invisible Committee argues. "What is presented everywhere as an ecological catastrophe has never stopped being, above all, the manifestation of a disastrous relationship to the world."[58]

To establish a new "relationship to the world" is to establish a new rhythm for society – one that recognizes our place in and dependence upon the common. Such a recognition comes along with a renewed sense of class conflict: our commonality is reclaimed in our declaration that "we are the 99%." This must be extended, however, in whatever ways possible, to the entire biosphere: our new relationship must be one in which not only are we, the commons, not exploited, but in which we *Homo sapiens* do not exploit and destroy the larger commons that is life on earth.

"It is not the system that is disintegrating," Levebvre cautions, "it is the illusion of a system and the illusion of a coherent rationality that are dissipated … It is the entire society that became vacant; and there was no one to occupy it."[59] When we realize that our economy isn't *in* crisis, but rather, that it *is* crisis; when we realize that what we have in common – the mass of us suffering through this life of devastation and distraction – is the fact that we do not have a place in the world as it is, that this world is not set up for us, but for a small, privileged elite; when we realize, too, that this world is an "illusion of a coherent rationality," behind which hides greed, self-interest, and a reckless disregard for consequences that borders on ecocide; then, *then* we begin to vacate this world – we take ourselves out of it, and find somewhere else, somewhere new – a new rhythm – to occupy.

★

Despite the ways that we talk about it, it is not a question of *making* change, but rather, of *facilitating* change. This is learning to recognize the new rhythms and allow them to be played out in their necessary variations and exploratory complexities and diversities (both strategic and tactical). Facilitating a revolutionary change means "reading" its patterns and allowing its productive tensions to drive it forward. One does not "control" or even really "foment" a revolution; one joins the dance, and facilitates the dancing of others.

I am using the sense of facilitation as employed in the Occupy movement's general assemblies. The facilitator is there simply to allow the voices present to be heard, and to help unveil the points of tension and the points of agreement. The revolution becomes general when we all take our turns, at different moments, in different contexts, and in different ways, as facilitators of the revolutionary change underway. We are participants who enable others to participate more fully.

★

Social change is never simple, and there are many versions of this picture, some of which the reader will find scattered throughout this book, but at this point, being as realistic a utopian as I can be, I would say that the global Occupy movement is:

The "demand" – if it is a demand – for system change, a wholesale rebuilding of our socioeconomic system, beginning right now. Until this process is seriously engaged, until all the 99% realize *they* are the ones suffering from the current system and simultaneously *the only ones* capable of changing this system, we will occupy squares and public spaces, creating new social rhythms, new definitions of daily life, spreading their resonances as we build a new world in the shell of the old. We can "demand" this change because we are now beginning to recognize that we can indeed *facilitate* this change – we demand it of ourselves – invigorated with a new confidence that we can begin to do this now, together, everywhere that we find ourselves.

The new world we are asking ourselves for is one of ecological and social integrity – one based on a new definition of "the common good": that which is of the highest value is that which is most common, most widely shared. In this new world, economics and ecology are consciously applied as the same science of balanced livelihood. In this new world a sustainable social metabolism is never sacrificed for immediate gain, and the common good is always truly what benefits the entire commons – in all its multispecies diversity.

The way to this new world is through a new political process – direct, horizontally dispersed, participatory democracy. We have taken our squares on this basis. Our form is our content. No one can stand forward and demand a greater share than any other. To begin, we organize ourselves from the bottom up. To begin, we throw corporate influence out of our political system, and return to the true definition of democracy: a social system of the people, for the people, by the people. To begin, we enter the agora once again.

We "demand" – once again, of ourselves and only ourselves – but for the entire planet and all the species upon it as well – a right to the future. A right to *have* a future. This is dependent upon a new, sustainable socioeconomic system today. We are a potential species – a species of possibilities. It is the source of our creativity. Without a future, there is no potentiality and no possibility – no creativity. We will not allow this to happen. We won't sell all our tomorrows for the lie of economic pragmatics (which is code for economic exploitation) today.

★

My hope resides in the attitude of countless young men and women – most of them in their twenties or early thirties – who have thrown themselves into the Occupy movement despite a whole host of difficulties and deterrents. My hope lies in their disproving the myth of apathy and laziness, the myth of a lack of commitment and the power of leisure. My hope lies – not so much in the commitment to technology ("the revolution will be tweeted") of this generation – but their sense that this technology is simply one manifestation of a networked view of the world, a horizontal and global world where the 99% strikes no one as an ironic or idealistic trope, and where, ultimately, technology is simply a matter of better tools for getting bodies into the street, quickly and en masse. My hope lies in the words of young people like Anthony Mayfield, a university student from Edmonton, Alberta, who, while studying in Vancouver, has thrown himself into this global social movement, heart and soul. I end this essay with Anthony's words, taken from a Facebook discussion, because they evoke the sentiment of so many people who still hold hope despite the almost total lack of hope, who continue to see potentiality in this era of narrowing potential:

> I'm confident that the system today is designed by a plutocracy for plutocrats, and that "the people currently in charge of things" are merely system

managers of a construction that is terrible for nearly every living thing on planet Earth, and planet Earth, but favors a sliver of society enormously. (Feudalism never died, it's on a comeback.) I'm also convinced that this is because of collusion between State powers and corporate and banking powers. I'm convinced because it's proven, and pretty objectively verifiable and observable.

I don't want to run anything. I just want a bit of fairness – I'm tired of nobody saying anything about this mass robbery/Ponzi-scheme that is being constructed into a security/surveillance State.

Whether or not our species is capable of change is beyond me. We might just be hard-wired to be absolutely fucking shitty and deserve the dumbed-down culture and incessant oppression by a bigger, more powerful ape. I don't know whether or not me toiling over this day after day is the right path or whether I should just shrug and accept that we're moving backwards and on a course with certain extinction, and then go play some basketball and drink beer and dance to shitty club music.

Basically:

Are we hard-wired to suck and incapable of change, or at least incapable of creating a force that can surmount the power and interests of Goldman Sachs?

or

Will computer technology and the aid of the network of the Internet allow us to harbor information technology, organize efficiently and free ourselves?

It's a toss-up.

But, meh, I already know my answer. Even if it's not worth it, and my toiling is all for not, I don't really care. I'll keep fighting and trying to mobilize my generation, if for no other reason than to know that I stayed with the fight until we lost. If for no other reason than to know that I wasn't like so many others who just gave up and lost confidence in themselves. I wouldn't be able to live with the hypocrisy of trying to ignite a flame of giving a fuck within my generation and then turn around and try and fade back into a menial, passive life. Even if nobody else hops on board I'll take the hard road myself, I don't have any dreams of a big car or a blonde, platinum wife with a baby. There may be no purpose to a life of resistance as it may turn out to all be for nothing, but regardless there is more purpose in that than just accepting that nothing can be done and giving up. My hand here is forced: I will continue to fight, even if it means my eventual burning out and perishing in a war of attrition against forces too powerful to upend. By this point, there is no value I can find in a cookie-cutter standardized life set out for me by State and corporate values … A life of resistance is my final choice.

PART 2

DISPATCHES FROM
THE OCCUPATION

PEACEFUL PROTEST
OCTOBER 15 2011
OCCUPYVANCOUVER
WE ARE THE 99 PERCENT
IF YOU CARE YOU SHOULD COME
IF YOU ARE HOMELESS YOU SHOULD COME
IF YOU ARE UNEMPLOYED YOU SHOULD COME
IF YOU LOVE THE PLANET YOU SHOULD COME
IF YOU HAVE A MORTGAGE YOU SHOULD COME
IF YOU HAVE BEEN LAID OFF YOU SHOULD COME
IF YOU HAVE STUDENT DEBT YOU SHOULD COME
IF YOU HAVE CREDIT CARD DEBT YOU SHOULD COME
IF YOU ARE AGAINST THE DRUG WAR YOU SHOULD COME
IF YOU HAVE BEEN A VICTIM OF CRIME YOU SHOULD COME
IF YOU KNOW MAINSTREAM MEDIA LIES YOU SHOULD COME
IF YOU SUPPORT OCCUPY WALL STREET YOU SHOULD COME
IF YOUR HOUSE HAS BEEN FORECLOSED ON YOU SHOULD COME
IF YOU THINK OUR DEMOCRACY IS BROKEN YOU SHOULD COME
IF YOU THINK ITS TIME TO JAIL THE BANKERS YOU SHOULD COME
IF YOU KNOW YOU CANT VOTE FOR REAL CHANGE YOU SHOULD COME
IF YOU ARE STRUGGLING TO PAY ALL YOUR BILLS YOU SHOULD COME
IF YOU HAVE BEEN A VICTIM OF POLICE BRUTALITY YOU SHOULD COME
IF YOU ARE CONCERNED YOU MIGHT LOSE YOU JOB YOU SHOULD COME
IF YOU HAVE BEEN DENIED A PENSION YOU DESERVE YOU SHOULD COME
IF YOU LOST YOUR SAVING IN THE ECONOMIC CRASH YOU SHOULD COME
IF YOU WANT TO TAKE PART IN A GLOBAL MOVEMENT YOU SHOULD COME
IF YOU HAVE A UNIVERSITY DEGREE BUT CANT USE IT YOU SHOULD COME
IF YOU HAVE A CHILD AND CARE ABOUT THEIR FUTURE YOU SHOULD COME
IF YOU ARE A SMALL BUSINESS OWNER WHO IS STRUGGLING YOU SHOULD COME
IF YOU ARE WILLING 2 DROP YOUR LABELS AND WORK AS ONE YOU SHOULD COME
VANCOUVER ART GALLERY · OCTOBER 15 2011 · IN SOLIDARITY WITH THE WORLD

YOU SHOULD COME AND JOIN US
OCCUPY VANCOUVER

Occupy Vancouver – We Move In!

The sun was shining, and by my guess some three or four thousand people were mostly smiling – as one sign said: "Nice Day for a Revolution." There were speeches, and there was a march through the streets of downtown Vancouver. Tents – only a few at first, but more as the day wore on – were pitched, in defiance of the bylaw signs clearly visible on the Vancouver Art Gallery grounds. Yes, the general assembly spent much of its time discussing what the correct hand signals were, and whether or not to use (a) the PA system, (b) the human microphone, or (c) a combination of the two (the latter mostly won out – interestingly, once you start shouting back what someone else has said, it's difficult to stop). Yes, there were lots of cops present, but they were mostly in the background, and while several motorcycle cops tried to stay in front of the march, they didn't "lead" or "contain" it, and often found themselves backtracking after the column made sudden, unpredictable turns. All in all, it was a celebration, really – an enthusiastic embracing of a new moment of potentiality – a hand reaching out to grasp a hand extended already in Madrid and New York City.

Was it messy? A bit. Chaotic? Sometimes. Frustrating? Often. But this is the nature of the beast (or, as the saying goes, what democracy … looks like). The Vancouver Art Gallery is now our agora. It is now the *commune de Vancouver*. No doubt it will take days, maybe weeks, for the general assemblies to start functioning smoothly, before consensus – that much-bandied-about term in these opening discussions – is actually found on a regular basis.

One critique of the Occupy movement, in these early days of its existence, has been its vagueness – its extreme openness and its refusal to establish goals and demands or sometimes even specific talking points outside of the process of consensus-based assemblies. One sign, to me, captured this sense of "general" disease: it simply read: "Down with That Sort of Thing." Down with *what*, we might ask? Whatever you happen to be down on, I guess, and there was a great variety to be "against" here – from the regulation of unpasteurized milk to the crimes of former US presidents, and genetically modified food to blatant examples of corporate greed.

I suppose all I want to say in this first post is: let's give it some time. Let's be patient. Let's stick with this. It's not always going to be smooth sailing (how do four thousand people have a conversation about real and pressing – and complicated – social issues, anyway?). It's not always going to be pretty. Or polite. Or always profound. But there is work to do – the work of actually making the important decisions for ourselves, with each other. And with a little effort, we might just get there – to the possibility of another, more just world.

Occupy Earth

Occupy Vancouver has produced a small city within the city – the kernel of a new world sprouting within the shell of the old. There's the "Education Station," complete with library (the new university); the first-aid shelter (hospital); the "Food Not Bombs" shelter (restaurant); and the tent city (urban sprawl). Everywhere you look, meetings are breaking out, forming, and disbanding as people leave one cluster only to coalesce into another. Calls of "mic check" echo every few minutes as information is shared. I asked – at the media tent – if people were reading the blog or following on Facebook. No, was the answer I received, there's too much happening right here! Reflection can come later. Right now, a new world is being fashioned.

This is Michael Kimmelman's point in one of the better pieces I've read on the Occupy movement. Kimmelman writes, "No matter how instrumental new media have become in spreading protest these days, nothing replaces people taking to the streets." "Politics troubles our consciences," Kimmelman goes on, "but places haunt our imaginations."[1]

The Vancouver Art Gallery (VAG) has become such a place. Perhaps my favorite sign – and there are a *lot* of signs, a whole cache of them piled up, the armory of this information-heavy war – is simple and subtle. It's just the word "occupy," in perfect cursive script, which someone has managed to stick to the granite side of the VAG, beneath one of the sculpture lions. The material the word in written in? Moss. At least I think it's moss. It certainly looks like it.

I suppose what this word fires in my imagination is a reminder of the convergence of economic (Occupy Wall Street) and ecological (environmental) concerns that have become increasingly inseparable in recent social movements. The very words "economy" and "ecology" share the Greek root *oikos*, meaning "home." So (simplifying extremely) "economy" is *how* we make our living, and "ecology" is *where* we make it. We are realizing more and more that how we make our living (as a species) is destroying where we make it (the web of other species – and this earth).

The VAG has been occupied. But the goal has to be a (economically and ecologically) better occupation of this planet. Once we fully realize that we are in occupation of an entire planet – that we have *filled* it with our presence like no other species ever has – then we can begin to work out the sustainable politics of this reality. Right now, we are living in denial of what this might mean.

All Power to the Occupations

So what *does* democracy look like?

Consider the usually accepted point of democracy's origin: in ancient Athens. Citizens met in the agora – an open space in the center of the city (it was also the marketplace) where everyone who participated in the decision-making process could see and hear each other. I'm not sure if they called out "mic check" when they wanted to speak, but something similar must have been the practice.

Of course, Athenian democracy – like all actually existing democracies to follow – was open to serious criticism. First and foremost, we have to ask who "participated"? Not women. Not foreigners (they were referred to as "barbarians"). And not slaves (that's right, the democratic Athenians owned slaves). So we're really talking about a small rump of the population having the right to democratic "privileges."

All subsequent democracies in history have struggled with this same problem: who's in, who's out, how is access gained to the democratic process, and to what degree can people "participate." Although democracies like ours in theory allow for full participation (everyone can vote, stupid!), factors such as income, gender, race, and the legacies of colonialism complicate it in practice. Money is the real key to the modern agora (which is even more so a marketplace than its Athenian forerunner), and we know how unevenly that is distributed.

Related to this is another problem: if democracy was "invented" in Athens, it was invented with the agora in mind: a system in which the participants could see and hear each other directly. Since those rosy days, no modern democracy has been that … small. All modern democracies make compromises forced, in part, by scale: when you have more people than can conceivably see and hear each other in person, what do you do? Elect representatives. Now, inequality enters the picture. The larger the agora, the more dispersed and dematerialized (virtual) it becomes, the more prone it is to inequality, and the more opportunity exists for abuse.

I'm writing this in the early morning on the steps of the VAG, looking down on our agora, where even now a few people gather in small clusters to talk. Later, the general assembly will convene and we will try to hear and see each other, en masse. We will practice a seemingly ancient form of direct democracy – really, one that didn't even exist in exclusionary Athens – one that has only broken forth in modern democracies a few times: the Paris Commune in 1871; the very early days of the Russian Revolution (when "all power to the soviets" actually meant "all power to the soviets"); Catalonia, for a few months in 1936; and maybe now, in a host of cities worldwide where Occupy has taken hold, echoing those earlier moments. At least, I hope that's what we're seeing. I hope that's what this could be.

But it's not a matter of repeating history. This thing, democracy, has some real power to it (!), but we've never quite got it right – not all the way, not for very long. Henry David Thoreau asks, in *Resistance to Civil Government*, whether we should really sit back and rest, satisfied that the democratic system we have evolved is the final word in social organization – "the last improvement possible in government," he writes.[2] The only true answer is: *how could we be so arrogant to think so?* What is happening in the various occupations right now is a retooling of democracy from the ground up. At least that's the potential – that's what's at stake. That's the challenge everyone seems to be eagerly taking up with each enthusiastic response to a call of "mic check!"

The Form *Is the* Content *(I)*

I find myself compelled to return to the question of the "content" of the Occupy movement: what are the "demands"? What do people "want" or hope to "accomplish"? Where are the "directives" or "measures" or even "recommendations"?

As I have said before, such questions miss the point. They are posed by the corporate media and State officials, because they think in terms of immediate and easy-to-process "outcomes" (not to mention a hierarchical "chain of command" where requests have to work their way up the ladder of power): they need sound bites to sell the news and buy votes. But here's the thing: in this movement, it's not that there's a lack of content (there is one hell of a lot of content, actually) – it's that the *form* of what's going on is (arguably) its most significant "content."

Or you could also frame this as process over product. I walk onto the site this morning. It's sunny, a day between rainfalls. People are wandering away from the Food Not Bombs tent with bowls of something warm in their hands, conversing in small groups. A larger cluster stands in the main assembly area – maybe just a dozen people – talking softly. There is always a group there – different people at different times of the day – discussing various issues. This morning the subject is the missing women's inquiry (a First Nations–led demonstration against the show trial–like and meaningless "inquiry" into police mishandling of a serial killer investigation) a block away at the corner of Granville and Georgia. Someone calls out "mic check" and the group and others nearby discuss heading over to support them (which they do). Elsewhere, committee meetings will be happening all day. And then, at one o'clock and seven o'clock, the general assemblies will draw hundreds into direct, face-to-face democratic discussion.

What is being discussed? Everything. Hand signals. Proposed direct actions. A proposed talk by a group concerned about Canadian mining companies. Tarps. Pallets. Poetry. The decision-making process. Inclusiveness. The missing women's botched inquiry. Sign painting and art. Music. Speeches. Anti-oppression. The economic structure of global capitalism.

At the GA the other night, a young man stood beside me, participating in the human microphone. He was sharply dressed, and his long hair was pulled back in a tidy ponytail. I think he was new to the occupation, as he started asking me some questions about what was going on. Suddenly he noticed the tents (it was dark now), and asked, "People are camping here?" "Yeah," I said, "lots of people." "Shit," he said with a grin, "I'm quitting my job and moving in!"

The form of what is going on here is based in part on participation, of course, but also on accumulation: of people, of places (how many occupied cities?), and of days. This is not a one-off protest but a movement. Accumulating spatially and temporally.

As the Industrial Workers of the World (IWW) proclaimed in their constitution, by "organizing," "we are forming the structure of the new society within the shell of the old."[3] You can see that going on, all over the occupation site. It's about relations, not (at least not at this point) "outcomes" or simply "content."

So far the tactics being used – "peaceful," non-antagonistic demonstration; patience; a relative lack of detail and specificity in the "message" broadcast to the "public" – seem to be working. Such tactics are keeping a State/media system used to direct and one-off protests off-balance. They aren't really used to something this large moving in and staying put, addressing itself to the general imbalances and structural problems of the whole "system," organizing locally but connected to the other occupations transnationally. But make no mistake (as the politicians love to say), push will come to shove in one form or another (see what happened early this morning at Occupy Oakland),[4] and other tactics may have to be brought into the fold.

Still, I hope the content and form of the movement will hold, even in more difficult phases of the process, and we will continue to build – even when confrontations come – the new society in our every word and act, in the relations we practice with every conversation.

Poem for Oakland

Dear menacing force
Smoke-eyed with your
Tear-gas canisters
Beanbag shotgun shells
And bullets – rubber
And otherwise – know this:
Crowd dispersal
Is just a phase in
Crowd formation –
Wherever you cut
A swath through this
Living mass you
Will find it has
Formed again on'
Other streets moving
Back into whatever
Space you've just vacated
And we will occupy
Once again.

Know this too:
In Oakland and New York
Vancouver and Toronto
We have learned
From our brothers and sisters
In Tahrir Square

The Puerta del Sol
And everywhere else
We've learned to say
Enough
And stare down
Riot cops and soldiers –
It will take more
Than a simple show of force
More than smoke mirrors
Concussions and noise
To chase us off now –
We are not satisfied
With a single skirmish
We are not satisfied
With one day of rage
We are in love
With this *we*
We are becoming
And we are coming
Oakland
We are coming
New York
And we have each others' backs

Whose Side Are You On?

In his article "The Crises of Democratic Capitalism," Wolfgang Streeck argues that as long as those two terms – "democracy" and "capitalism" – are uncomfortably yoked together, the political system will to a certain extent struggle (unsuccessfully) to satisfy (let's not say "meet") the needs of both public and private interests.[5] Politicians need votes, so they have some (limited) pressure to respond to the needs of at least some portion of the 99% (the "democratic" side of that ledger), but they are obviously financially at the whim of the 1% (in terms of direct financial influence, but increasingly, in terms of national debts and large-scale economic policy, which obviously impacts the 99%).

This side of the 2008 economic crisis, things are even worse, and we would need to situate the Occupy movement in this context: government debt leaps up via bailouts that in turn have the beneficiaries of those bailouts – banks – putting the screws to governments to service their increasing debt (they now owe the banks money for the banks' misdeeds!) by instituting austerity measures. Vicious circle, anyone? The result, as we all know, is the rich get richer and the poor get poorer. Democracy goes (even further) in the tank as the 1% has governments by the … you know what. When the 99% feel (a) economic pressure, plus (b) the erosion of their democratic rights (that is – when it becomes *glaringly clear* who is making the decisions and for whose benefit – spoiler: it's not us, not for our benefit), they do the only thing they can. They take to the streets.

This little bit of political economy is really just a way of framing a very local question facing Occupy Vancouver, and which has been much discussed on-site and online in light of the attack on Occupy Oakland and the ratcheting up of the rhetoric about the occupation in the Vancouver mayoral race. The question is this: whose side are the City and the cops going to be on? Mayoral candidates are savvy politicians who are testing the waters of voter opinion on the occupation. They have "democratic" interests – in the distorted way democracy now functions (which boils down to: "What do I have to listen and respond to in order to get enough votes?). But they also know who they ultimately "serve": an influential 1% concerned that Vancouver appear "open for business" and compliant when difficult measures (cuts) and the generally decaying condition of the economy erode the quality of life for the 99%.

The cops, as many have said, may be (in terms of their paychecks) part of the 99%. But they are also the means by which compliance is ensured and the "Open for Business" (read: investment) signs are maintained for the benefit of the 1%. They will do what governments tell them to do, who in turn do – increasingly, in these economically fraught times – what the 1% tells them to do.

But – and this is the source of the energy circulating through the veins of the Occupy movement – *we are the 99%*. It might not be a totally accurate number. And we might chafe against being defined as an abstract percentage. But it points to the glaring fact: the majority is being told to stuff it, while the smallest minority is making profits like never before. The majority faces the brunt of State violence, while the truly criminal 1% escapes prosecution and enjoys protection. Governments and cops might be caught in between – but they know where their paychecks come from. They know that, when the chips are down, capitalism (the 1%) trumps democracy (the 99%).

The question is – will the numbers game matter to them? Can the 99% throw the weight of their numbers around to any effect? We'll also have to ask ourselves, as the weather gets colder and the city gets meaner and the politicians argue over the best strategy to clear the VAG: whose side are you on, boys, whose side are you on?

We Demand We Don't Demand Anything (Yet)

On Saturday, I attended Toby Sanger's talk on the Robin Hood Tax at Occupy Vancouver and I participated in the march with my two daughters. It was all pretty low-key – a street party, really (the band was, as usual, a lot of fun), with a few memorable moments (such as Eric Hamilton-Smith's impassioned speech outside the Industry Canada and Services Canada offices at 300 West Georgia, complete with Leninesque pose). Hundreds of us marched and chanted and sang, blocking traffic and carrying signs – doing what occupiers do as our almost daily practice.

What I like about the Robin Hood Tax campaign is that it offers a simple, straightforward "demand" – a 1 percent (or less) tax on all currency trading and speculative financial transactions.[6] Because the volume of such trading is so immense, the tax would generate a substantial amount of money to be directed toward social programs, effectively replacing what is being lost due to austerity measures forced upon people by those same financial powers and their government debtors. It is also in some ways a more "realistic" goal, because it has some "high-level" support: France's Nicolas Sarkozy and Germany's Angela Merkel have voiced support for the tax (though Canada's Stephen Harper is a vocal opponent).

With all the rhetoric around 99% versus 1%, a 1 percent tax has even more symbolic traction, seemingly concocted for the occasion (though it's actually been around for some time). I don't have a problem with it and would support it. But here's the issue: it's yet another plan to make adjustments to the system that we increasingly realize is fundamentally broken. It keeps the current system tottering along – and while it redistributes wealth to some extent, it's still just skimming 1 percent off the 1%.

Making demands is, to some extent, part of the old politics. It assumes there is some (potentially benevolent) power to whom demands can be made by people far less powerful. One can't really demand that there be nothing to demand, or no one to demand things of. But this is what's happening in the Occupy movement – we are demanding another world – we are demanding the impossible. Slavoj Žižec is right when he says: "Remember that our basic message is, 'We are allowed to think about alternatives.' If the rule is broken, we do not live in the best possible world."[7]

There's the key demand – the first real demand, from which we can begin to build others. We demand an alternative. We demand to be able to take time and talk, to figure out what a *real* alternative might be. To work at it, from the bottom up, in tents in the middle of our cities if need be. Capitalism isn't built for this, however: it's built for efficiency. It requires a top-down structure, because it needs to move quickly, to react to markets and "volatility." We demand that we don't move quickly anymore. Moving quickly has got us nothing but environmental destruction, social and economic inequality, and exploitation. Tar sands and pipelines and climate change. Massive corporate profits for the 1% and diminishing expectations for the 99%.

I don't know how we can avoid making demands in the long run, but a clear sign that we need to be cautious is the mainstream media's appetite for such demands; they know the drill: give us your crazy, your idealism, your impossible, your fringe. We know where to put it! Front page, with the other entertainment, to be replaced by some other scandal tomorrow.

I've been thinking a lot about the 1871 Paris Commune these past few weeks, and about the many parallels it has with the occupations. Both represent an experiment in direct democracy amid economic and authoritarian pressures. In the midst of a seemingly hopeless situation, there is the discovery of some fresh reserve of hope – an imaginative leap toward another world. The parallel is even more poignant when thinking of Oakland and other occupations that have faced police violence and the State's brutal response. Change is as much about repetition as it is about difference. But things *do* change. We come around to the same historical moment, and realize we've learned something. The tools are different, too. Maybe they will work to our advantage this time? "Now the field is open," Žižec says. Let's see if we can keep it open. Let's see how far we can stretch its boundaries – before it breaks. Let's make a big demand – change everything – and have that be our starting point for any "negotiations" that may occur.

Right to the Future

We have to assert – for *all* members of our species, and especially for *all* other species, too – an inalienable *right to the future*.

I'm working from, and simply expanding a little, David Harvey's notion of a "right to the city." He writes:

> We live in an era when ideals of human rights have moved centre stage both politically and ethically. A great deal of energy is expended in promoting their significance for the construction of a better world. But for the most part the concepts circulating do not fundamentally challenge hegemonic liberal and neo-liberal market logics, or the dominant modes of legality and state action. We live, after all, in a world in which the rights of private property and the profit rate trump all other notions of rights ... The right to the city is far more than the individual liberty to access urban resources: it is a right to change ourselves by changing the city. It is, moreover, a common rather than an individual right since this transformation inevitably depends upon the exercise of a collective power.[8]

The right to the future is similarly a "common rather than an individual right." The right to the future is crucial now, when young people feel exactly this: no future (to quote the once-again-relevant Sex Pistols). A right to the future needs to be asserted, not just to give young people hope (though we need that), not just to press our demands for a better world, but because this is exactly what human beings – perhaps all species – are not naturally very good at: taking future consequences of their actions into account. And our system – economically and ecologically – is suffering most acutely from endemic shortsightedness. Profit today, when this might make the market crash a few months or years down the road? Hell yeah! The environmental consequences of what we're dumping in the ocean? I won't be around to see it wash back ashore! We live like Jerry Seinfeld's TV persona, who, when taking one of those "don't pay a cent until June" deals, shrugged and said, "June! It'll never be June!" I'm sorry, Jerry, June has arrived – in October.

Harvey, writing in 2008, goes on to ask, "Where is our 1968 or, even more dramatically, our version of the Commune?" I think he'd recognize it now in the Occupy movement. Indeed, in a recent blog post on the Verso Books website, he writes of the challenges facing the occupations:

> All this has to be democratically assembled into a coherent opposition, which must also freely contemplate what an alternative city, an alternative political system and, ultimately, an alternative way of organizing production, distribution and consumption for the benefit of the people, might look like. Otherwise, a future for the young that points to spiraling private indebtedness and deepening public austerity, all for the benefit of the one percent, is no future at all.[9]

This is what the 99% can and should be demanding: a right to the future, which means a real share in the outcomes of present surplus and accumulation, a more equitable role in deciding what our futures might look like, a promise of real ecological sustainability so we can inhabit a biologically diverse and healthy world, and, yes, hope, and possibility, and the rich potentiality that life should embody. This is why I'm involved in Occupy Vancouver.

I have heard people say we don't have it so bad in Vancouver – it's not like Egypt, or Greece, or even many parts of the US … Tell that to the Downtown Eastside (Canada's "poorest postal code"). Tell that to the families of Vancouver's missing women.[10] Tell that to the developers reaping extravagant profits, and the many who pay more than half their incomes for housing. Tell that to the Vancouver-based mining companies whose profits soared while the markets shuddered and tailing ponds and effluent poisoned rivers and lakes. Tell that to the unemployed and the deeply indebted, the students shuddering under the burden of their loans and the cost of living and studying in this city. Tell that to the elderly and those living on fixed incomes. Tell that to the many First Nations whose traditional lands have been *occupied* – without treaty or compensation – for decades now while their standard of living has spiraled downward as the settler's city arose around them. Vancouver is becoming the crown jewel of income disparity. It is a property speculator's paradise. And it is in need of a better future – a more accessibly and equitably shared future – as much as anywhere else.

Let's get down to the tents and assert our collective right to the future, here and now.

The Form *Is the* Content *(II); or,*

Don't Take My Tent, Bro!

So the fire department showed up today to check on the tents. I think Occupy Vancouver's response was great: we don't recognize your authority over this space, and we've begun our own restructuring of the tents, anyway, thank you very much. The idea that Occupy Vancouver is "unsafe" or "unhealthy" is ridiculous. There are health and safety issues *everywhere* in Vancouver, but what you'll find at the occupation site is a community dedicated to mutual aid and respect. We're looking out for each other, which is more than the City does on a regular basis (consider the problems of homelessness, mental illness, and drug addiction writ large and you'll see what I mean).

The decree against tarps is the leading edge of the City's attempt to dismantle Occupy Vancouver. Step 1: get the public worried about health, drugs, "crime," safety, civic image, etc. Step 2: demand that the encampment be rearranged or "cleaned up," and partly dismantled on this basis (really, "opening up" the tent encampment is another way of enabling surveillance and "emergency access" for the city – you know where this leads!). How "open" does it need to be? How "clean"? It is a tent city, remember. People are camping in the heart of the city.

The problem isn't health. It isn't safety. It's authority. It's power. It's a matter of who gets to make the decisions and how. What the City of Vancouver needs to remember is that it, too, was once a mere tent.

Mayor, Council, and City officials
assembled in front of a tent, 1886.

CITY OF VANCOUVER ARCHIVES
(CVA 371-2570)

City Hall & 1st Council 1886

This is exactly what they are worried about – that we'll do the job better for ourselves than our affluent, "professional," developer-influenced "representatives" are currently doing "for us."

The tent is crucial. The word, the idea, "occupy," like everything else in this movement, is a holding-open gesture, a tactical resistance to quick resolution, a recognition that the space our current problems "occupy" is *everywhere*, unresolved, difficult to nail down because it is so *general*. By "occupying everywhere" we are taking up this space. The tent is our key symbol in many ways, the way the red flag, or the barricade, or Lady Liberty were in past struggles. The *tent* – because we are moving in, setting up camp *in* the space of this problem. The *tent* – because the runaway real estate market, property, housing, homelessness is very much the issue here in Vancouver. The *tent* – because better to camp, temporarily, than for anyone to act like they *own* this place.

Which brings us back around to that word "occupy" again. The question might be framed like this: is "occupation" the same as "colonization"?

There are a number of reasons to question the appropriateness of calling this movement an "occupation." For First Nations people, the occupation started a long time ago – thus the use of this word by a movement for social justice understandably doesn't sit right with some. How about "Unoccupy" (they are trying that in Albuquerque) or "Preoccupied" or even "Decolonize Vancouver?"

Although I'm not sure we should get stuck on terminology at this point, I believe it's crucial, "foundational," as a friend of mine says, for the acknowledgment of unceded aboriginal land to be the starting point of *all* social movements here on this coast where a colonial history of theft and murder underlies all that has happened since. We must account for this history, and allow it to inform everything that Occupy Vancouver does – and becomes. (We haven't done a very good job of this so far, but I hope that we are getting there.)

The real traction, and the original idea of the "occupy" movement, was in *what* was being occupied: not a university president's office or some government ministry or a vacant lot awaiting development or even this very real public square (as in past occupations), but *Wall Street*. All of it. Its centers and its

dispersed tentacles. The very *concept* of the financial sector of the economy generally. How does one "occupy" capitalism? Clog its metaphoric and ubiquitous office entrance? Where do you throw your tent?

It's a matter of the form being the content once again. Physical spaces are occupied, yes, but what is really being occupied is an idea, an all-pervasive structure, an economic system gone haywire, a society (and, particularly, marginal groups within that society) that doesn't get to participate in making the decisions that affect it most. In this movement we are everywhere and nowhere, occupying the city and the imagination – just like the system we are working to oppose. We are "occupying" the very political process. We are trying to show how it might be taken back. As the movement has moved from city to city, it has taken on a particular identity that we cannot separate from the word "occupy" now. We really are indeed "occupying everywhere."

In the end, I think we're stuck with the word "occupy" for now, the benefits of which – as long as we don't lose track of very specific, local, foundational contradictions in the word – outweigh the problems. But only just. The name is there, and has rapidly become a fixture in public consciousness. But don't forget that *this* occupation comes on top of *those* other occupations, and must stand in solidarity with the displaced, not the displacers, not the act of displacing. Every morning that people walk the block from the art gallery to the missing women's protest at Georgia and Granville, they take a little bit of the stain off that word "occupy." If every time we say, "Occupy Vancouver" we are reminded that Vancouver is already occupied – has been for over 125 years – and if we factor this into each movement we make toward equality, solidarity, freedom, and the fashioning of a better world out of the ruinous contradictions of this one, then we might just be all right. If we continue to push for inclusiveness, to allow space for (and bring) other voices into the committees and assemblies at Occupy Vancouver – even when this means that the ubiquitous white male must take a step back for a moment – then we can put this on the right track, and the contents of an inclusive society will follow the forms of inclusiveness we build.

Tragedy on the Commons

Yesterday, a tragedy occurred. A young woman lost her life. We do not yet know the cause of her death (she was found unresponsive in her tent, late in the afternoon), and speculation without facts is both irresponsible and reckless.[11]

At a brief press conference on-site last night, Vancouver Police Department (VPD) spokesperson Jana McGuinness said as much: we don't know the facts yet, and we should not speculate. Mayor Gregor Robertson then spoke, and indeed speculated – or at least drew conclusions based upon speculation: Occupy Vancouver has "deteriorated" and "there are real questions now as to safety on this site," he claimed. He then called for the immediate removal of the occupation.

Robertson's willingness to jump to conclusions, when the VPD spokesperson would not, highlights the difference between a politician and a civil servant. For the politician, in the midst of a re-election campaign, this tragedy can be used to achieve political ends: the removal of the encampment, and thus the satisfaction of a vocal part of his constituency (revealed in recent polls – also a factor in the mayor's willingness to move toward confrontation, no doubt).

If conditions are "deteriorating" and becoming "unsafe," then they are so for *all* of Vancouver. The occupation is simply a micro-cosm – a lens that is bringing a number of issues into sharper focus. Some of these issues include extreme poverty, homelessness, mental illness, and drug addiction. These issues are not exclusive to the Occupy Vancouver camp. If they are cause to shut down the camp, then they are cause to shut down *all* of Vancouver. These issues *should* make us worry; they are indeed signs of deterioration – but that deterioration is endemic to Vancouver in this moment, to global capitalism in this moment, when so many people are being thrown under the wheels of profit, development, and growth. These issues *are* the issues Occupy Vancouver is trying to bring to wider attention. The economic system is failing us; living conditions for too many are "deteriorating"; the political system is unresponsive.

Robertson's response to yesterday's tragedy is an easy out: blame the systemic problems on a small encampment that is coming under increasing media and political attack. Are some people both inside the movement and watching it from the sidelines becoming frustrated with Occupy Vancouver? Yes. And it's no wonder: we're trying something here that hasn't really been tried in this way before. It's characterized by dispersed, non-hierarchical decision making and open participation. Views expressed will sometimes be contradictory, and sometimes it won't be clear who is speaking on behalf of what constituency. It will take time, and it will take up (public) space. This is certainly not business as usual.

The City and the media have become antagonistic. They are using this tragedy as ammunition against the occupation, and against the issues the occupation is trying to address. And the response at Occupy Vancouver? Grieving. Love. Solidarity. Heavy hearts, but continuing determination. In the name of this young woman, Ashlie Gough, we cannot stop now.

Turning Tides and Sacred Fires

Feeling a bit darker now – antagonistic media hounding for comment and response – the city around us seeming angrier, frustrated to the point of belligerence with these *annoying protesters*. It's never been easy to stand up and call for change. As so many other people involved in this movement are finding, we are learning *how* to do this every day. Every day my approach changes a little. Every day I find I have fallen down and must pick myself up, dust myself off, and feel a little more humility.

The occupations everywhere began by asking for change and for patience – because, clearly, change doesn't come quickly or smoothly. The issues we face (an increasingly lopsided distribution of wealth and power, collusion between corporate and government "leaders," rapidly eroding world ecosystems) are huge and complex – and they demand some response, but the existing system is failing miserably. Occupiers promised non-violence and open dialogue. Things moved along quite well for the first few weeks here in Vancouver – though many were impatient, and many, both inside and outside the movement, wanted to hear demands and concrete plans, or for the protesters to just hurry up and get on with it – still a majority of people were probably sympathetic.

Then the first overdose. And then Ashlie's tragic death. It's not even been a week yet – but that moment seems to have changed everything. The media, the City, large parts of the "public," too, suddenly felt the whole movement was simply about drugs, dropping out, and causing havoc. The occupation was "unsafe" and "unhealthy" – and though I have seen no concrete evidence for this claim (that is, no evidence that suggests the occupation is *any more* unclean or unhealthy than other places where marginalized, homeless, and addicted people live in Vancouver – in fact, in this context, it is decidedly safer and healthier), it has risen to the level of a metaphysical truth about the protests writ large: they are not "safe" or "healthy" for this society. And more and more people agree: *we can't change anything – look how dirty and dangerous change is – just give up – come on, we have nice coffee, movies, video games, skiing – stop all this pointless complaining!*

Do we have doubts? Yes. Do we hesitate, unsure what our next move should be? Of course. Do we make mistakes? You better believe it – we're figuring something new out, a new process for the political, and it will make a mess at times. But there will be a next move. There will be a continuation of the Occupy movement—because it *is everywhere*. It is a global movement. And this is where things have stalled in Vancouver.

Tents are not the point – despite their symbolic value at this point in time. The whole world is our tent, flapping and fragile in the winds of this historical moment. The occupations are global – in thousands of cities all over the world. In each city the global issues we share (largely economic and ecological) play out a little differently as they interface with local particularities. In Vancouver, the movement has become ensnared in those local particularities – the housing problem, homelessness, drug addiction especially – as well as the civic election and the ongoing issue of unceded indigenous land. These are very real and significant issues, obviously. But they are also local manifestations of a global pattern and problem. And in Vancouver – in a few quick days – things have turned and we have lost sight of those global issues. Attacked from the outside, some occupiers have grown more agitated in their responses, some have turned on each other, and we all lose sight of what's really at stake.

Bill Tieleman, in an article in that paragon of journalistic integrity, *24 Hours*, calls Occupy Vancouver a "sad parody of a revolution."[12] In any revolution, there will be moments of parody, and moments of sincerity. Moments of conflict, and moments of peace. There will be antics, and brilliant new tactics. The media is painting the entire movement the color of its moments of parody, conflict, and antics, and ignoring its sincerity, peace, and tactics. Perhaps this is to be expected. But I will never stop insisting that at the core of this movement, there is generosity, good intent, a will to change the world for the better, and a desire to have *all* share both in this process, and in this better world.

The day after Ashlie's death, Michael Stone spoke at Occupy Vancouver.[13] He reminded us that this is not a protest, but a movement; that we do not have new demands, but a new process. As a society we've suffered a failure of (the political) imagination, Stone went on, and the occupation is about creating a space for imagination. He also noted that such movements must work from compassion, and they do so by gathering and caring for the outcast – the seemingly unkempt, "unsafe," "unhealthy." In caring for each other, occupiers in Vancouver have somehow drawn this city's ire.

I share Michael's worry that "when you leave here, you'll forget this movement transcends this park." We may indeed have to leave this space, but will we be able to "transcend" the grounds of the VAG? That is the real question here: the City and the media have tried to limit the issues to this one space. And we have, probably mistakenly, agreed.

One characteristic of the Occupy movement *everywhere* has been its compassion and humility. If the people of Vancouver feel that the movement here has made mistakes and created problems, I think this is the sort of movement that will rise above these errors, will compassionately embrace them and redress them, and will move forward, better and stronger for having failed, but persisted. That's where my hope lies now. But hope is a fragile thing – like a tent.

Last night, as First Nations elders tended a sacred fire in memory of Ashlie – in an oil drum away from any flammable tents – the VPD and fire department chose to force their way in and douse what was little more than a source of some smoke around which people peacefully prayed. The tides are turning indeed.

Video footage and numerous eye-witness accounts testify to the fact that the tiny, ceremonial fire was set safely and tended by a large crowd surrounding it. The intent of such a fire is not heat, and not spectacle. Its intent is to smolder, the smoke from its sacred wood cleansing this site and everyone on it.

At one point a TV news crew, apparently "tipped off," arrived on-site, and I happened to be the first person to speak with them. Eagerly, they inquired about the fire. I led them to the drum. "*That's it?*" the reporter asked incredulously. "That's it," I said. She huffed and wandered off, her camera crew in tow.

Bites, Lies, and Videotape

I'm writing today with one simple purpose: to counter VPD Chief Jim Chu's misinformation regarding the sacred fire incident on Monday night at Occupy Vancouver.

Jim Chu would have us believe that, as fire fighters attempted to put out a fire in a barrel, VPD officers came "to the aid of fire personnel." In the ensuing scuffle, an officer was kicked and bitten. This, Chu contends, is a sign that a "violent element" has "infiltrated" Occupy Vancouver.[14] Chu has ordered all city personnel to stand back (there have been police officers, fire personnel, and city workers on-site since the occupation began), perhaps as a precursor to forcibly removing the occupation.

Here are some facts. Things did get rough that night, and they escalated quickly. But let's be clear: they escalated only when the fire personnel, and then police officers, tried to force their way to the fire barrel, which occupiers and First Nations people were (non-violently) protecting. The police began to throw people to the ground and shove them away from the fire, which was eventually doused and removed by fire personnel.

And what about that fire barrel? It was a sacred fire started by First Nations elders to ritually cleanse the site where there had been harm and even a death. Carefully set and tended, the fire smoldered for many hours before the eleven o'clock assault. Fire personnel were in attendance throughout, and were in fact consulted several times. At no point did they indicate there was a problem.

And what about that bite? Today I spoke to the biter. She is a calm, well-spoken and educated, elegantly dressed woman in her forties. Perhaps best described as "new age," she exudes peace and calmness. Here is her version of the incident: tending the sacred fire that night, she saw a VPD officer throw a slight, young woman from the melee onto the ground – *hard*. Instinct, perhaps, took over and, outraged, this woman slapped the officer across the face. The officer then grabbed and twisted her wrist. Panicked and in pain, the woman kicked the officer, and yes, she bit his hand. The officer then let go.

At last night's general assembly, Occupy Vancouver agreed to accept most of the fire department's safety recommendations. Occupy Vancouver also re-affirmed its commitment to non-violent protest. There is *no* "violent element" at Occupy Vancouver, nor has there ever been. There is only the tendency to instinctively strike back when attacked. There is also compassion and resolve. The issues that have brought this encampment together, this movement into the streets, have not been dimmed. The fire in our hearts and minds has not been put out.

Why did police officers and fire personnel decide, after many hours of peaceful gathering and prayer around the barrel, to forcibly extinguish a fire that they had earlier determined posed no threat or harm? The word "provocation" comes to mind – it certainly has allowed Jim Chu to wash his hands of the whole affair, and declare Occupy Vancouver a dangerous menace.

Yes. Be careful. Some of us bite when beaten.

But seriously, something very ominous has happened here. First Nations people everywhere should be, and in fact are, outraged by this attack on their ceremony. *Everyone* should be outraged by this attack: it lacked reason and respect, and showed only brutality. But what does the City want to focus on? A woman, who bit a man, who was hurting her.

Spirit of the Occupation

Two great responses yesterday to Vancouver's media-driven and ill-informed turn against the Occupation:

> [Michael Stewart:] The explanation for this turn-about is simple: those who continue to occupy the art gallery lawn are activists, community organizers and volunteers who have been plying their trade in the Downtown Eastside for years. DTES residents and their allies have been marginalized, alienated, vilified, and victimized by the city and its citizens as a matter of course for decades. They gained purchase on mainstream discourse through the 99 per cent, who supported them so long as the political invest-ment was minimal. The tenters disproportionately shoulder the injustice perpetuated by the one per cent, and now they find themselves in a familiar po-sition: abandoned by a well-meaning majority who finds their poverty distasteful.[15]

> [Geoff Olson:] Without actually conversing with the regulars at the art gallery grounds, it's easy for cyn-ics to frame the scene as a disorganized collection of druggies and thugs, when actually some of our city's best and brightest are still active there. Examining it as a whole, in all its contradictory parts, Occupy Vancouver is the elephant in the living room – both

a reminder and a response to a broken system. We can shoo it off or shoot it dead, but the social problems feeding this unpredictable pachyderm aren't going away soon.[16]

These articles are excellent assessments of the core of the socio-economic issues at hand, and of the frightening mob psychology of the city's rejection and demonization of the occupation. My own contribution to this much-needed defense would be to focus on the continuing spirit of the movement, which I think is best exemplified by one simple incident from the GA a few nights ago.

In the middle of a discussion, an angry voice began shouting from somewhere in the gathered crowd of more than one hundred occupiers. Some people moved toward this person and began talking to him while the main discussion continued. Then this smaller group interrupted with a point of process and – despite diverging from the current topic – asked to let the dissenter speak from the stage. He was allowed to do so, and took the mic.

He was an older man, and he was obviously agitated. He leaped right into the typical rant – *you are a bunch of worthless, drugged-up hippies – stop ruining my city and get a job, etc.* A few catcalls and shouts were returned, but other members of the assembly quickly called for quiet and respect. When the man was finished, several young people escorted him from the stage and sat down with him off to one side while the GA continued. A half hour later, I noticed they were still in quiet and calm discussion with the (formerly) angry man.

It is this spirit of openness that continues to light this process that amazes – despite all the pressures, attacks, misinformation, suspicions, and potential divisions. How different from mayoral debates or House of Commons discussions is this? It would be of no account in the mainstream media that occupiers were willing to welcome, listen to, and converse with their critics and dissenters – because they are entirely focused on another agenda: writing off the movement before they've really listened to it. That same media claims it's the movement that has abandoned the 99%. In fact, much of the 99% remains on the fence, as they long have been, awaiting the next development.

From what I have seen, for every one person who is given over to rage or frustration, ten or twenty are there to calm them and keep the peace. But the pressures are huge. We are losing good people on all sides. Maybe the ship is going down. We have to remember the spirit of openness and inclusion that this moment began with, in the sunshine of the VAG steps. It's that spirit that the ethos of competition driving capitalism has long been trying to crush.

Occupy 101

What follows are notes toward – what? A manifesto? A list of demands? Not really. These are simply summaries of my thoughts and impressions about the Occupy movement as I have watched, participated in, and speculated about it over the past four weeks. Call them this professor's outline for an "Occupy 101." There's a lot more nuance to these issues than I go into here – but I'm trying to be schematic, conceptual. I hope the following three points will be useful in the ongoing and collective attempt to "explain" the movement – both to those of us involved in it, and those who remain skeptical or even antagonistic to it.

1.

The problems we face in the world today are diverse, wide-ranging, and complex. But here's a useful (I hope) shorthand that takes us right into the heart of the matter, and that shorthand is found in the nexus formed by the words "economy" and "ecology." Both derive from the Greek *oikos*, meaning "home." Simply put, economy is *how* we make our living and our home; ecology is *where* we make our living and our home. Obviously, these two concepts need to be in harmony and balance. But today they are not: our economy constantly and often excessively damages our ecology, and we value making a living far and above ensuring the sustainability of the places in which we make that living.

Our global economic system is based on, driven by, and in need of constant growth. Like a shark, it dies if it doesn't keep moving. Or better, like cancer, it only knows growth, regardless of the consequences for its "host." As long as GDPs keep rising, it doesn't matter how unequally distributed that wealth is, how badly people suffer, or what happens to the environment. So our *economics* ignore and surpass all limits. But our *ecologies* are all about limits – each ecosystem is limited (by climate, geography, resources, etc.), and the ultimate limit is the earth itself, the entire biosphere. Our current economic system has run right past these ecological limits (the excess registering in global warming, the extinction of species, the loss of the world's forests, huge Texas-sized patches of plastic floating in our oceans, etc.). In Slavoj Žižec's analogy, we are like Wile E. Coyote, running off the edge of the economic/ecological cliff. When we finally look down, we'll fall.

2.

The Occupy movement is a response to just this situation. But what is that response? It has confused many people, because it starts from this position: the problem is vast; I don't presume to know the solution; I don't think *you* know the solution – *no one* knows the solution. So let's sit down together and try to figure it out, because collectively, by really engaging with these problems and listening to each other, we might find some new solutions.

This is a different model of politics than we're used to. Normally, we have a consumer-driven notion of politics: voting (or deciding to attend or not attend a one-day demonstration, for that matter) is a bit like shopping. "Will I have a lager or a pale ale?" "Will I buy the red one, or the blue one?" The Occupy movement represents a non-consumerist form of politics. The normal electoral process is for the most part dispensed with (it really only serves, as the mantra goes, the interests of the 1% who dominate and benefit from the current economic system). Consumable outcomes like demands (which might be set before that existing but malfunctioning political system) have largely not been produced. *A different form of daily life*, of relating to one another, is what has been produced. This is a movement, rather than a protest, because it is extended spatially (in thousands of cities at once) and temporally (the occupations are ongoing, announcing no end point) in ways that most past movements for social change have rarely been able to achieve.

Another way of looking at this is to say that the Occupy movement is more about *form* than *content*. We don't know what the content of a new, better system might be yet, but we're willing to try a new form for getting there, and take up the time and space it requires to figure this out. This form is the ongoing, open, inclusive, horizontal, everyone-has-a-voice general assembly that lies at the heart of all the occupations. "What do you want?" people (in the media, especially) keep asking. The answer is that we want to talk. We want to listen. We want to find new ideas for organizing our world socially, politically, and economically – because what we've got right now isn't sustainable, isn't remotely equitable, and just isn't working anymore.

3.

If we were to imagine a "demand" coming out of the Occupy movement, it would be a general demand for a universal right to the future. The collision of our unsustainable economic system with the very real ecological limits of this planet is depriving us all of this: our right to the future. A right to the future means a right for each of us to as long, healthy, and fulfilling a life as possible. A right to the future means a right for young people to imagine having children one day, if they so choose, and for those children to have as long, healthy, and fulfilling lives as they can. A right to the future means that each and every species on this planet has a right to live out its normal life pattern as evolution, not human intervention, dictates. This is what I think the Occupy movement stands for. This is the most basic thing any of us can ask for: tomorrow, and a tomorrow after that tomorrow. Hope. A future of possibilities. This is what is at stake. We have created a world that burns its tomorrows to feed the unsustainable fires of today.

We demand a better world. We demand a more inclusive and peaceful world. We demand a more sustainable world. There. I said it. Now let's figure it out.

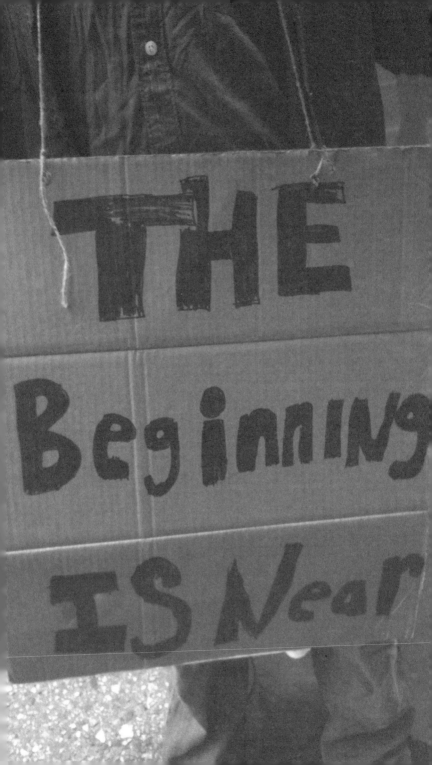

A History of Change (I): Solidarity Forever

To brothers and sisters at Occupy Wall Street, Occupy Oakland, UC Berkeley, Occupy Portland, and other cities where occupations have come under attack in recent days: love and strength. We know you will be back – you already are – even stronger and more determined than before. To brothers and sisters in Toronto and Calgary and other cities – like Vancouver – under threat of eviction: love and strength. We know you carry on under the threat of State violence, and we know that, no matter what, you will carry on through the days and months ahead.

I have solidarity on my mind today. To that end, I want to briefly address the question of divisions within the movement – mostly idle but nonetheless increasingly damaging talk of "reformers" versus "revolutionaries" or the "compliant" versus the "defiant" camps. If these fractures have even formed at all, it is *only because of the intense pressure of the State to do away with Occupy everywhere.* We are all stressed. We might begin to see bogeymen where our comrades once stood. Don't. They are more than likely our allies. They want change, too.

I'll say this flat-out: *all significant historical movements in favor of profound social change have had more* and *less "aggressive" wings, more* and *less "confrontational" formations. And it is because of this very tension between radicals and reformers (for lack of better terms) that these movements have been significant and have been profound.* Without this tension, these movements would not have been successful to the extent that they were, and we would not now have the benefit of their achievements.

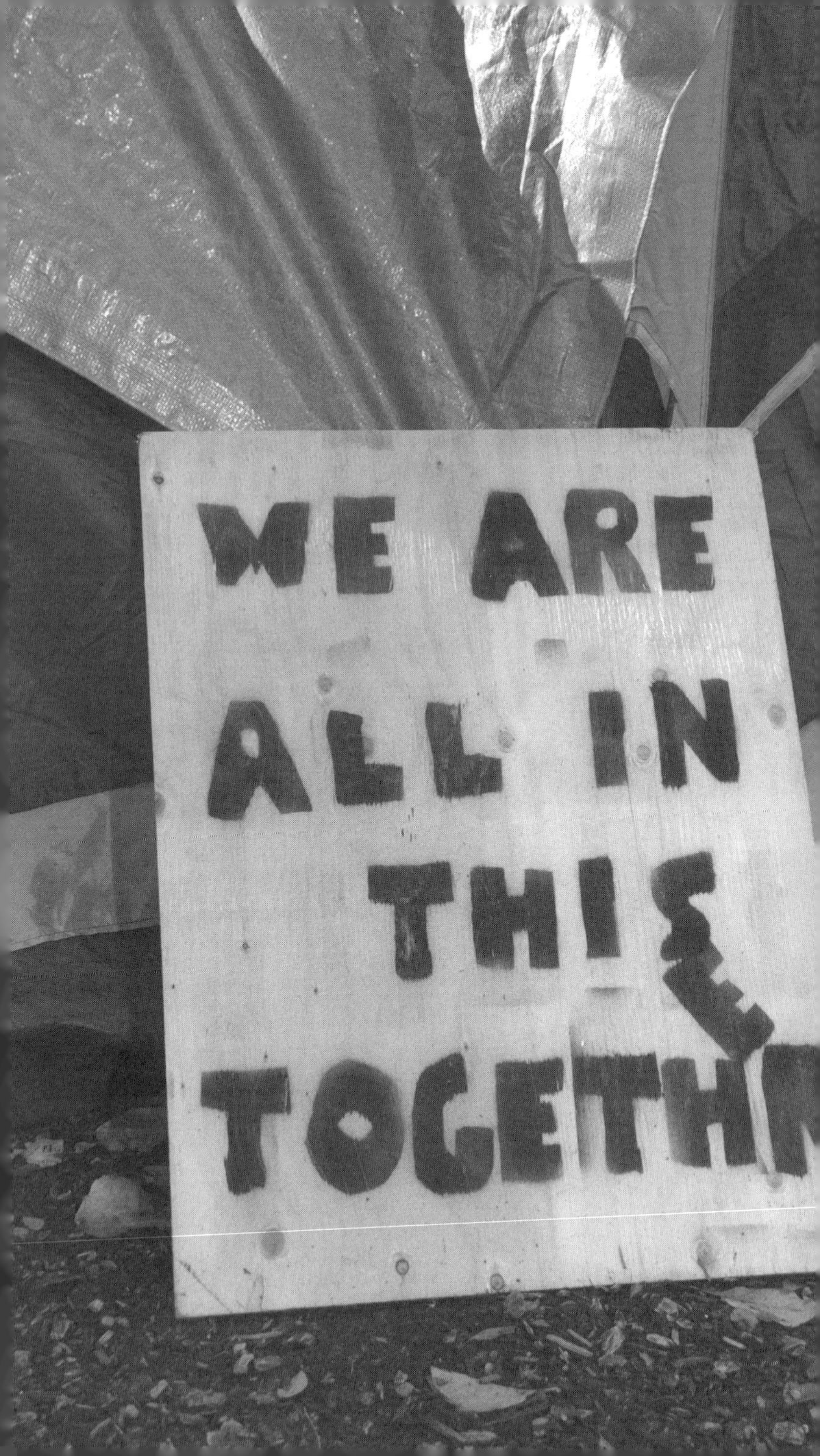
WE ARE
ALL IN
THIS
TOGETH

Think: what would the civil rights movement have been without Martin Luther King's Southern Baptist movement *and* the Black Panthers? Or early-twentieth-century labor struggles without "progressive" political parties *and* the direct actions of radical unions like the IWW? Or nineteenth-century Parisian revolutions without Republicans *and* insurrectionary Blanquists?

It is in the dialectic of these tensions that change (from which the entire 99% can benefit) occurs. We have to see the big picture. Does this suggest a "diversity of tactics"? Only to the extent that one does indeed see diverse groups engaging in diverse tactics in each and every significant historical social movement.

Perhaps those people who want to talk about division are just shit-disturbers. Maybe they are infiltrators, bent on fostering just such internal divisions. I don't know, and in many ways, it just doesn't matter. For now, what's important is that we put our visions of fifth columns and renegade cadres aside. We need solidarity right now. We have pressing work to do on the vast and complex problems we all face. We need a clear message to the world: we are many, we are working toward change that can benefit all the 99%. We have hope and we have tenacity – join us, for our cause is yours!

A History of Change (II): The Question of Cities

On November 17, while as many as thirty thousand people marched through downtown New York in support of OWS, here in Vancouver a smaller group marched from the Vancouver Art Gallery along Georgia Street to the Royal Centre, where Brookfield Properties have second-floor offices. Brookfield, as many now know, "own" Liberty (Zuccotti) Park, the once-and-future home of OWS in Lower Manhattan; they, along with other members of the corporate 1%, pressured billionaire mayor Michael Bloomberg to evict OWS on Tuesday morning. In Vancouver, we tried to bring the fight to Brookfield, occupying their lobby and forcing the building to be locked down.

Brookfield casts the issues the Occupy movement raises in an interesting light: it is a Canadian-based company, "one of North America's largest commercial real estate companies," as their own website trumpets, one whose "holdings" became the epicenter of, first, a local act of civil disobedience in New York City, and second, of a global movement for social, economic, and political change. Thus far, the Occupy movement has been characterized by this duality: it is a movement of particular cities, in particular urban "public" spaces, and it is a movement of the global city, writ large.

I can understand why the Occupy movement is focused on the struggle for public space in city centers – cities are, after all, hubs of accumulation and financial trading in capitalism. What is more puzzling, however, is why the debate *about* the Occupy movement has been "contained" (by State and media apparatuses) at the level of the city (rather than, say, the level of the province/state or nation). Noticed any commentary on the movement from those levels of government? Me neither. The silence is telling.

Containing the "public" debate about the Occupy movement at the civic level allows officials to approach it as merely a question of public "health and safety" and "sanitation" (the grounds civic governments have most often cited for the removal of occupations). It reduces the occupations to matters of zoning and bylaw enforcement – as though it's just another permit decision along the lines of parades and public sporting celebrations. (Note the discussion here in Vancouver about whether the occupation can legitimately inconvenience the Santa Clause Parade, or what effect it will have on Grey Cup celebrations, as though they are comparable spectacles!)

Brookfield enters the issue here, too: as a commercial real estate developer, their main interaction with governments is at the city level (through project development applications and building permits). But again, hiding behind mere "locality" here is the issue of the global city: Brookfield is active in the contemporary city writ large, Vancouver, Toronto, New York, and beyond – wherever capital is accumulated through property speculation. It builds the spaces the corporate 1% inhabits, and profits along with them. In addition to this, its investments in resource extraction also point to the tangle of contemporary capitalism, where "money" (that increasingly abstract and hypothetical measure of "value") cycles through urban development, rural resource extraction, finance capital, debt servicing and restructuring, and government coffers – back, forth, up, down, and sideways – just not through the hands of the masses.

If higher levels of government entered the debate about the occupations, they would thereby acknowledge that the movement is in fact a provincial/state or national issue. It would take its place beside other "big" issues states have to deal with. Occupy would no longer be a mere question of "health and safety," but a question necessarily about the very "state of the union" – the social contract itself, the meaning of "representation," the relation of economic development to ecological degradation – everything the movement is *trying* to talk about.

But something else is revealed here: the redundancy of those higher levels of government. New, post-national and transregional levels of government are being engaged in the Occupy movement as mayors and police chiefs enter into intercity discussions about how to deal with the multitudinous occupations (as Oakland mayor Jean Quan recently revealed),[17] just as the Occupy movement itself has intercity committees sharing information and organizing expressions of solidarity between cities.

What does all this tell us? It's probably still too early to say for sure (and time may reveal how much federal governments were in fact involved, behind the scenes), but it suggests two, probably fairly obvious, points of entry for further thought.

First, in terms of the (at least momentarily) "federated" structure of civic governments, it's clear that the task of enforcing the compliance of the 99% with the dictates of the 1% is demanding the coordination of policing at a level, and in a way, we have not really seen before in North America. Police tactics have been increasingly "paramilitarized," and we are more than ever before staring in the face of a coordinated global "state police" (and police state) whose main focus is going to be dealing with civil disobedience. This has been in the planning stages for some time, in anticipation, no doubt, of pushback against austerity measures – and is only now really being tested for the first time outside the parameters of a G8 or G20 demonstration.

Second, in terms of the Occupy movement itself, resistance and civil disobedience are similarly taking on decentered, "federated" structures where tactics and resources are shared and expressions of intercity solidarity are as important as intracity ones. This is, in part, to say that if civic governments and police forces can "federate" to coordinate their activities (however centralized such coordination may be, behind closed doors), then so can and do the various occupations – both of them, note, appearing to operate outside the sphere of the normal centralized State apparatus.

Another way of putting this: at the level of civic governments, the State's dirty work is being downloaded and outsourced (as it almost always is); at the level of the occupations, well, this is a revolution. The shell of the old world is resounding increasingly hollow, as it throws more and more police into the echoing streets.

We are indeed "occupying everywhere." But the fact that those "everywheres" are particular cities is crucial – because the city is where we gather to debate what is and is not a just society. And this debate is not simply a matter of elections (Oh, Vancouver, this day of our own civic election): it's a matter of a return to where the real "demand for justice" is made – in the agora. I will end here with a passage from Luc Boltanski and Eve Chiapello's *The New Spirit of Capitalism*, which considers the connection between the city and justice (and to which I will return below):

> The concept of the city is oriented towards the question of justice. It is intended to be modeled on the kind of operations that actors engage in during disputes with one another, when they are faced with a demand for justification. This demand for justification is inextricably linked to the possibility of critique. The justification is necessary to back up the critique, or to answer it when it condemns the unjust character of some specific situation.[18]

Our End Is Our Beginning

Occupy Vancouver is being evicted – but as they have said in New York, "you cannot evict an idea whose time has come." We will continue to occupy everywhere. We will occupy the places where people meet and speak, travel and rest, stand and gather in Vancouver. If there can be no designated agora, we will make everywhere we are, at any given moment, an agora. We will do so politely but persistently, non-threateningly but urgently. We will approach our fellow citizens and invite them to engage with this "idea whose time has come." We will listen and we will offer our opinions. We will respect others and be open to all. But we will occupy. All of Vancouver is a space for general assemblies.

We will occupy because it is clear that the way we are making our living is destroying the ecologies in which we live. We will occupy because profits are everywhere being put before people. We will occupy because we all deserve bright tomorrows, not diminishing returns. We will occupy because we love this world and the people we share it with, and because we think that we can all, working together, find new solutions to the pressing problems that our broken system has to this point failed to fix.

We, average citizens of average North American cities and towns, have been politicized and socially engaged by the events around the world – by the people of Egypt and Tunisia throwing off their totalitarian regimes, by the people of Europe resisting draconian austerity measures, by the threat of such measures, and by the spiraling personal debt and financial need – experienced by more and more Americans and Canadians (while "too big to fail" banks reap the benefit of tax-payer bailouts, and the largest corporations pay little or no taxes but exercise unequaled political influence). We have been politicized and socially engaged by OWS – by the beauty and civility of inclusive discussion and the direct democracy of general assemblies – and we have been politicized and socially engaged by the repression of OWS, Occupy Oakland, and the brutal assaults of militarized State police on peacefully demonstrating students in California. We know we can change the world now, because we know we *must* change the world now. We have no choice. The masks are off. Brutality will retreat everywhere. We will press our case, arms linked in an endless human chain.

People say, "It's not so bad here in Canada – it's not the same as in the US or Europe – you don't have anything to complain about!" In truth, the situation in Canada is headed in exactly the same direction as the rest of the world: it's a global economy, and economically, things are getting worse, the divide between rich and poor is getting worse, people's standard of living is getting worse, our natural environments are getting worse.

The Occupy movement is global. It was always bigger than an encampment of tents at the Vancouver Art Gallery. We will continue to take care of our poor and homeless, feeding and housing them – make no mistake. But we will also keep to the larger task at hand for all responsible citizens of the world: protect the environment, work toward sustainability and equality, remove the influence of money from politics, give everyone equal access to a healthy, creative, balanced, and fulfilling life.

This is our one request: that we be allowed to be fully human, that we live in peace, equally sharing and caring for this planet and each other. It is a big thing to ask. But we ask it for all of us. We hope you will join in the struggle to realize it – we're all counting on it, in fact. And we aren't going anywhere – because we are everywhere.

A History of Change (III): Tents Not Guns

Reflecting on yesterday's relocation of the encampment, after we spent the morning tearing down tents and platforms and marching through Vancouver's streets with domes and tents held over our heads, only to land our new camp right on top of the law courts that granted the injunction to evict us from our first camp, I thought about our transition to a new, possibly nomadic, occupation.[19]

And I thought of the Zapatistas in Chiapas, Mexico. The Zapatistas seemed to step unannounced out of the Lacandon jungle on New Year's Day, 1994. They stormed several towns by force, fought the Mexican army, made declarations, and then disappeared back into that same jungle. Ever since, they periodically reappear, take actions and make statements, and carry on their struggle for equality, dignity, justice, and indigenous rights.

The Zapatistas are a different sort of revolutionary movement: they claim to have no interest in taking power or imposing a new program; their "demands" are broad, global, and ask for real and fundamental change in the world – for justice, dignity, and sustainability. Their desire is to create "a democratic space, where the confrontation between diverse political points of view can be resolved."[20]

The Zapatista rebellion begins with the cry, "*Enough!*" "We rose up," their spokespeople declared, "so that they would listen to us."[21] At the center of this movement's decision-making process is the village assembly, where all take part.

Much here seems familiar. We, too, have risen because no one in power was listening – and they still aren't. Today's *Province* quotes Premier Christy Clark: "I don't know what these folks stand for now." She might have a better idea if she had attended our press conference yesterday, read a few blogs, or watched a few videos.[22]

We, too, will rise, occupy space, fade into the streets, and occupy another space – and another, and another. Why? Because we want a real "democratic space" for direct discussion of the key economic, ecological, and social issues we collectively face.

I return to Boltanski and Chiapello's words with which I closed the last "History of Change" piece. The "concept of the city," they say, is built upon "the kind of operations that actors engage in during disputes with one another, when they are faced with a demand for justification." The City of Vancouver, and now the Province of British Columbia, is doing its damnedest to close down this "concept of the city," replacing it with a concept devoid of justice – one open only to property speculation and corporate sports spectacles. Occupy Vancouver – Occupy Everywhere – stands for just this (take note, premiers and prime ministers): a space of debate as an engine for change.

So we carried our tents to a new camp, and we will carry them again if we must. Unlike the Zapatistas, we don't have guns – just tents. We have committed ourselves to non-violence.

But don't be fooled by our tenting: we aren't campers who have lost our way to the Pacific Rim Park; we aren't "only" homeless (though many of us are, thanks to this unequal economic system).[23] The tent is our revolutionary symbol. In nineteenth-century Paris it was the barricade; in the 1960s it was the freedom march, a wall of demonstrators with their arms linked. For the Zapatistas, and many subsequent anti-capitalist demonstrators, it was the balaclava. Now, for us, it is the tent. Because the way we are running things in this world, the best home any of us may be able to count on will be a tent on the edge of some desolate wasteland.

Let's not let that happen. Let's occupy together.

Occupy Vancouver: Where Were We?
Where Are We Now? Where Are We Headed?

1. WE BUILT THIS CITY

A few days now separate us from the tents at the Vancouver Art Gallery, and as I look through the several hundred (mostly lousy iPhone) photographs I took over the thirty-eight days of the physical occupation, I'm overwhelmed with both sadness and joy. We built this – and we lost this. But what was it?

A beginning, for sure. Like the first note of a song, which your mind instantly tries to identify. Now we're anticipating the next note. But what I want to call it here – perhaps contrary to what many would think, even contrary to reason – is a utopia. An impossible, ideal city (which just happened to be built within the condo-lined walls of a less than ideal city). But this was no completely imaginary, far-fetched utopia, floating in the air or on some distant planet. This was that rarest of rare things: a "real" utopia (rare since by definition utopias are not supposed to be "real").

I'm calling Occupy Vancouver's VAG encampment a utopia in the full knowledge of all its problems and failures – that there was mess and confusion and chaos at times, that people suffered and died there, that people argued and disagreed and went away from there angry, that many, many people now feel dissatisfied with both how things went down, and where we are now – chased into the alleys and parks and suburbs looking for shelter.

I'm calling Occupy Vancouver's VAG encampment a utopia in the particular terms offered by David Harvey in *Spaces of Hope*, where Harvey calls for a "dialectical utopia."[24] Harvey, arguing for the necessity of a return to utopian thinking (in a bid to find and create new alternatives to capitalism), cautions that such a return cannot be based upon old utopian models of perfect societies in distant, "undiscovered" lands or worlds. Rather, utopian thought must work dialectically with actually existing conditions, in very real and particular (and problematic!) built environments.

This is what I would focus on in my post-camp assessments: we built a small city within a city, and did the "work" of cities. And we did it for free, as volunteers, and we did it often better than the moneyed city did. That's the utopian part: we spent thirty-eight days mostly trying to help each other, and make the world better.

This city we built provided free "housing" to those who needed it (tent city), free meals (Food Not Bombs), and medical services. This city we built had a library, a teahouse, an elders tent, and a media tent – in all of which the open, intellectual exchange of ideas was a main activity. This city we built established an agora where general assemblies engaged daily in the processes of direct, open, and transparent democracy.

This is also to say that the VAG occupation was an experiment: what if we put the free, open exchange of ideas and political debate at the center of our societies (which is to say, what if we actually *performed* democracy)? What if being citizens meant just this: participants in self-governance?

The utopian aspect of the city we built was also to be found in its inclusivity and diversity. Those largely excluded and marginalized in Vancouver found themselves welcome in Occupy Vancouver. They found themselves heard and they discovered that their opinions were not only valued, but also depended upon. Again, I know each individual experienced Occupy Vancouver differently, but by and large this is the most common experience I found others expressing: sheer joy and excitement at being included, at experiencing – perhaps for the first time – a sense of collective agency, at being part of a process that valued individuals and worked toward collective goals.

The City of Vancouver's first line of attack – health and safety – was a smoke screen and diversion. Any city – utopian or otherwise – encounters problems that it must solve. Occupy Vancouver encountered problems and it found solutions. "Health" and "safety" at the camp – if measured only in the City of Vancouver's terms ("cleanliness" and "accessibility") – was at a very high level, all things considered, over its final few weeks, as attention was increasingly brought to bear on these issues.

But the real issue always was the fact that Occupy Vancouver was a city within a city – and not just any city, but an inclusive city based upon the common in the midst of an exclusive city based upon the private. And that private city could not by definition allow that common city to exist in its midst – because the latter city contradicts the very basis of the former city's existence.

In other words, the City of Vancouver correctly identified what Occupy Vancouver was: an alternative, and thus a threat. What we're talking about is revolution. But it's a different sort of revolution.

2. OPERATION REBOOT

The real question that Occupy Vancouver was seeking to answer, then, was, how do you make a revolution here and now, in these North American conditions? How do you make a revolution in an advanced, "democratic," consumer society – *and fundamentally change that society?*

Clearly, methods that have been employed elsewhere in the world and history don't work in this situation. It's nearly impossible, for instance, to subvert a modern capitalist democracy by force – its ability to lull, pacify, divert, and purchase its citizens is unparalleled in history, and it has made itself the only legitimate employer of, and has monopolized the use of, force – its governments taking the mandate of an electoral victory as justification for any number of unilateral, aggressive, and sometimes very undemocratic actions. This is not the same case with dictatorships and authoritarian regimes, where "legitimacy" is almost always at issue (the conflicts at Tahrir Square, for instance, have been a great deal more violent than those in North America – and the tactics employed by protesters have been a good deal more diverse – because the regime's legitimacy is indeed at question). But note, clearly the government of a contemporary "democratic" State acts no less unilaterally and aggressively when perceiving an internal threat than does a dictatorship (as seen in the use of excessive force and militarized policing of protestors in recent years throughout North America – as well as in the erosion of civil liberties now being enacted through the courts of most so-called democracies).

Clearly – even momentarily setting aside ethical questions – non-violent resistance is the only real *tactical* option for us at this point, even as States move to outflank these tactics, pushing us to develop new ones again. What we need, as ever, are numbers in the streets, peaceful resilience and strength, and a common cause to generate those numbers. We need a population that has awoken from its consumer sleep. We need the realization that this, what we have now, is *not* what democracy looks like.

What we need to do right now though is pause – here in this post-tent, we-just-got-chased-off-and-have-to-regroup-and-lick-our-wounds moment – to look carefully at the reaction to our wild gambit of building a tent utopia here and now. What are the dangers we face now in this moment of transition?

The first danger is that Occupy will be co-opted. Our consumer culture has shown no limits in its ability to turn anything into a "market" or marketing strategy. We want to change in the world? The LED display on the Shell gas pump where I filled up the other day read: "Help us change the world." Shell is changing the world? Sure, environmental degradation, unsustainable resource extraction – I suppose that's a kind of "change." But it's obviously a travesty, and a complete abuse of the sort of "change" people would like to think they are contributing to via their consumer choices. We have to be careful about overusing the word "occupy," and beware its appropriation by consumer culture ("come occupy our new spring cars!"). If they try to "occupy" this word – that is, if corporations and media try to use it for their own frivolous ends – we will need to occupy them, swiftly and directly.

The second danger is that we will be ignored. The mainstream media and the many who follow its party line will simply move on to the next "big story" and refuse to cover Occupy anymore. They will say it's yesterday's news, the old story, just another moment of protest that finds its place in the long line of (the media would say mostly forgettable) protests. We need to resist this by keeping our movement in the public eye, even if there are necessarily "cooling-off" periods, while we recharge before emerging once again. We also need to keep developing and producing our own independent media – as the mainstream media begins (and has indeed already begun to) blackout anything to do with Occupy.

The final danger is that we will either implode (mainly via internal divisions and infighting – some prompted by external pressures, some by internal subversion) or – perhaps worse – as a means to avoid such an implosion, we will take on a more formalized and recognizable structure: say, that of a political party or NGO. I call this a danger because the strength of the Occupy movement is in its *formal* difference from past political movements (more on this below) and other already existing lobbying institutions, and because, once it takes on a recognizable *form* for which the State has pre-established protocols for dealing with, the game will be up – we will have created nothing new, and therefore no real change.

I suggest three strategies we should focus on in the interim, to help navigate these dangers.

1. We must maintain some sustainable version of our occupations. Continue the work of committees and the GA (though possibly shifting slightly to a spokescouncil model).[25] Organize several teams to carry out rolling, temporary "pop-up" occupations. The main goal here would be outreach: in each location, provide food and information to all and any who happen by, and hold a GA with local communities (or whoever just happens to be there) – inviting them into, and educating them about, the process of direct democracy.

2. We need to focus on our own media efforts. Keep getting our message out there. Create, gather, and distribute good and consistent content on the movement. Do not allow our cause to fall

off the radar, and do not allow some externally generated version of it to dominate. We have much to learn about doing this, and it should be something to which we devote considerable resources.

3. We need to teach, train, and support each other as we plan for and build toward a boisterous return to new "occupations" (whatever they might look like) and actions – coordinated globally – in the spring or fall ahead. When the movement explodes on the global stage once again – stronger, larger, and more focused than before – then, then we will be getting somewhere. That might take time. We need to start working toward it today.

3. THE REVOLUTION IS LOVE

I'm probably a fairly average sometimes activist. So I don't think I'm alone when I say that what I've struggled with for so long is that the problems we face are so vast and varied and multifaceted, I simply didn't always know where to begin. What part of this huge mess do I grab on to? With Occupy, we know where to begin. We begin everywhere and anywhere, right here and right now, with the very core and base of the problem: the whole economic system itself, which only really serves the wealthiest (who have direct and disproportionate access to the political, media, and State apparatuses) and which is dependent upon unsustainable environmental degradation.

What we learned from Tahrir Square was simple: urgency. Why wait? Why wait for someone else, smarter and more capable than us, to figure it out? Why wait until we have the credentials, or the solution, or the numbers, or the "leaders" to tell us what they think the "solution" is? We can't wait. And we can't depend upon our "leaders." Enough is enough. Start today by gathering at the center of our cities, by essentially "going on strike from one's culture."[26] We all know what's not working: the regime. Let's call for its end – *now* (not when the next election rolls around – we know what a con that is, for a change of government is *not* a change of regime under capitalism).

This is how we make a revolution now, in the Western world we live in. It is interesting that we had to learn this from the East –

that resistance to "dictatorships" can teach a new way of resisting the ossification of "democracies." The Occupy movement is about opening a space in our cluttered and careening midst for real thinking and discussion – *here* and *now*. It's about stopping what we've been doing. It's about stopping in the middle of our culture to sit down together, face to face, and ask, "Is this really what we want? Is this doing us any good?" Because this system always demands speed, forward movement, acceleration, we are not allowed to stop and ask why. But this is what we are doing – and this is the door we're kicking down in this new revolution. We are taking the time and creating the space to consider the world we want to live in – not the world that the wealthy and powerful want, which they perpetually proffer to us like the most able and persistent of salesmen (when they aren't simply forcing it down our throats with the mantra that *there is no alternative*, and marshaling the police to ensure we concur).

So the revolution, now, begins with stopping in the midst of the current system – of sitting down in its midst to say, "Enough of this. It's not working, it's not equal, and it's not sustainable." But it's what goes on in that space we create by hitting the systemic pause button that is crucial for understanding what this revolution will be about. We talk, and we listen. We share, and we begin to care for each other. We recognize our shared humanity and our shared distress. We give, according to our abilities, and we receive, according to our needs. We put an end to the domain of the private (in the sense of the individual's ability to "capitalize" personally on opportunity), and we open the domain of the common (in the sense of the community's ability to prosper through sharing and caring).

This revolution, then, is about love.

Michael Hardt and Antonio Negri introduce love as a political concept in their book *Commonwealth*: "When we band together, when we form a social body that is more powerful than any of our individual bodies alone, we are constructing a new and common subjectivity" – thus "love is a process of the production of the common."[27] But love, Hardt and Negri note, is mostly experienced in corrupted forms in our current society: love of the same (the people who are, safely and xenophobically, "just like us"), or a commodified "romantic love" as peddled by Hollywood movies and consumer culture. The political love Hardt and Negri are talking about is one that promotes "the encounters of singularities in the common" – a love that is the "motor force of association."[28] Here is the "force" this revolution can deploy against the armed "force" of the State: we cannot beat it on its terms – it has all the batons, pepper spray, and guns – but we can beat it by the force of our association together. This is what the State fears: that we will find each other, and support each other. And this is indeed what we've begun to do.

The space we have opened in the Occupy movement – the space of tent cities and especially general assemblies – is the space of love and the common. It is "always open, constitutive, and horizontal" and "legitimated by the consensus of singularities and the autonomy of each, in a relationship of reciprocity and collective self-rule."[29] This, at least, is its potentiality. And it reminds us once again of something important about *this* revolution: it's less a matter of demands, programs, or policies; more a matter of holding social space open for something new to start taking shape – or as I've already said, it's more a matter of *form* as opposed to *content* at this point.

Whatever does begin to take shape in terms of new programs or policies will have to come out of this new way of doing politics: out of love and the common – out of the consensus structure and process of the general assemblies and their associated committees. Or else we will indeed merely "reproduce the system" we are "trying to change," as Don Hazen writes:

> Of course, nothing concrete has changed, yet. But the possibility of change – really, the necessity of change – is now in the middle of our nation's politics and public discourse. This alone is an incredible achievement because a few short months ago, many millions of us essentially had no hope … [T]he OWS operation seems like the "wisdom of crowds" combined with a fundamental sense that top-down power can't really ever change anything, because it will always, by its nature, reproduce the system it is trying to change.[30]

As we catch our breath here, after this first two-month sprint, this is what should give us courage: we've found the right way to make a revolution now – it's through love, and the production of the common. Now, let's get down to the work of making it happen.

What Is the Idea Whose Time Has Come?

One of the most powerful slogans to come out of Occupy is "you cannot evict an idea whose time has come." I love this stirring conceptual meme (the phrase apparently originates with Victor Hugo). It points, for one thing, to the fact that this movement is more than tenting in public parks; it's about a conceptual shift in the underpinning ideas of our society – a shift that has caught on, and will survive the eviction of the physical encampments. But it does beg the question – what *is* this idea whose time has come? Answering this question goes some distance toward answering the common criticism of the Occupy movement: "we don't understand what you want!" This is to some extent understandable, as the idea whose time has come is a very big idea, with many facets and consequences. This idea signifies such a fundamental shift in thinking that it is no wonder people scratch their heads a bit. We have the meme. Let's start the process of fleshing out its meaning. As we do, we will find this idea keeps unfolding in deeper and deeper layers.

The idea that we can and should *care* **for each other and the planet.**[31] *Care* is at the meeting place of *love* and *responsibility*, and as poet Robert Duncan once said, responsibility is the exercise of our ability to respond; when we do so out of love, we are "caring" (as a verb: "to feel concern, be concerned; to take thought for, provide for, look after; to guard and preserve"). What a different political and economic system it would be if we would truly work from and through this idea! Capitalism is built on self-interest, competition, a lack of ongoing connection between social actors, and a seemingly "valueless" bottom line (profit and growth above all else). The intersecting economic, ecological, and political crises now shaking capitalism have the same root: greed, the pathological idea of unlimited growth, and the tendency not to see someone else's problem as our own – the idea whose time has come holds first and foremost that the days of apathy and not caring are over. Caring implies stewardship and trusteeship. It invokes our shared responsibilities for the one world we all coinhabit.

The idea that it is up to us to make the changes that need to be made – not up to some supposedly better-informed "expert" or supposedly more qualified "leader." We can and must all stop now and figure this out together, pooling the common resource of our collective intelligence; the idea whose time has come is that *we can do this* – the "Obama factor" (for all the disillusionment and failed promise of Obama's presidency, his message of change and his simple mantra, "Yes We Can," have resonated far beyond his ineffectual and in fact damaging administration).

The idea that we must fundamentally change how and what we are doing – because the *how* and the *what* of the current system have led to a completely dysfunctional, unbalanced, and unsustainable relationship between the economic, environmental, and social spheres. This idea also includes the concept, very active in the movement today, that another world truly is possible (and thus the idea that we must once again take up the project of utopia and activate our imaginations to envision and build that "other world").

The idea that we have a right to a future – that the current system is eroding and in fact robbing us of all our tomorrows in the name of excessive profits and unsustainable lifestyles today – that we have to act now, with considerable urgency, to ensure that we have a viable, bearable, and equitable future for all human beings, and indeed a world of balance and health for the entire biosphere.

The idea whose time has come? **What hurts you hurts me, and what heals you heals me. It's time to let the healing begin.**

Occutopia: Seven Visions of a New Society

Naomi Klein, speaking to Occupy Vancouver media in early December, put it this way: you can't just be "against," you also have to be "for" something. "The key is to interfere with the message that we have no other choice."[32] We need an alternative, a sense of what that "other choice" might be.

The Occupy movement has thus far been flooded with new ideas about and new energy for social organization and collective decision-making processes, and it has done an able job in weaving together a number of strands of critique – economic, ecological, and political – into a complete refutation of the current ailing socioeconomic system. What the movement has *not* produced much of yet are visions of what we might want to build, work toward, or replace the current system with – what we might imagine we'd like to change our world *into* when we call for social, economic, and political change.

Looking ahead to 2012, here is a glimpse of the world I would like to see us evolve toward – a vision perhaps for the year 2022 (or perhaps 2032) – but which we must begin transitioning toward in 2012. The Occupy movement, or at least the forces for change it is unleashing, can be the real driving force behind this transition as it formulates its vision and strategic plans and draws a wide array of activists and activist organizations together. Indeed, this is my vision of the world Occupy could help build – the extension of the movement outward to include all society and social production.

But this is not by any stretch of the imagination a fully fleshed utopia – just a sketch, structured around a series of conceptual nodes. I would like nothing better than to spur others on to think and imagine the details of a utopian, yet realizable, world they might also like to live in. In most respects, I see this sketch as fairly realistic and achievable. Honestly. I'd call it a "dialectical utopia," using geographer David Harvey's notion of a utopia based on real-world parameters, limits, and specifics (i.e., no spaceships or miracle cures) – but still asking for what often seems "impossible" and "fantastic" from the perspective of a present moment conditioned by the refrain that there is "no alternative" to the status quo.

VALUES

Society's core values are grounded in the idea of the common – not upon notions of economic or monetary "value," "growth" and expansion, or competition and individualism. We care for each other, the planet, and the future. Society bestows prestige on individuals who make exemplary contributions to the commonwealth (through cooperative social and community projects, for example) and "performance" and "innovation" are understood in terms of what makes the world better for us all, better for all species, and better for future generations. Our economy is modeled on the "gift economy," in which those who give the most to the commons are the most honored members of the community – although, because the focus on the commons is an end unto itself, everyone is seen as a vital contributor to the common good. Consumption is no longer the driving force of social life: we are learning to live with, and thus want, *less*; we give, we share, and we care for the commons that embodies us all and the entire biosphere. We understand that we cannot consume or hoard too much, as doing so harms the commons, and thus harms ourselves.

POLITICS

In "BC," as elsewhere, the only real "governments" in existence (the apparatus with which all real, significant decision making takes place) are community and neighborhood general assemblies and spokescouncils; there are also city-wide spokescouncils with term-limited and rotating "spokes" from the community GAs, but there is no city-wide GA – real, direct decision making can only function at a manageable, local scale. There are no parties, no "elections," no centralized governments at provincial/state or national levels – just biannual special regional spokescouncil meetings across broader, economically codependent regions (for example, "BC," or what we now call "Western Canada"). Thus corporate or financial interests don't influence the political system. Members of city-wide and special regional spokescouncils receive modest stipends and serve under strict term limits; these positions are open to any serving members of local community GAs. First Nations communities have full autonomy and occupy much of their traditional lands. Each traditional nation has its own spoke at the special regional spokescouncil.

ENERGY

Our dependence on oil, coal, and carbon-fuel production is minimal. The scar that was the tar sands is slowly being reclaimed by wildflowers and lichens. Renewable, sustainable solar, wind, and geothermal energy (which is abundant in BC) feed the economy now. We need and use *less* energy because our economies have been relocalized (we are growing upward of 90 percent of our own food), and because we are no longer dependent upon energy sources that themselves demanded intensive energy inputs to extract. Our carbon output has been cut by 70 to 80 percent from levels of only a decade ago.

ECONOMY

Global trade is limited to specific metals used in the production of technological equipment. The economy is largely based on local production and regional trade. Because of the changes in energy and trade, *less* energy is required, and consumption levels are far below those of the late twentieth and early twenty-first centuries.

Many energy- and resource-sector jobs have been replaced by jobs in renewable energy sources, infrastructural projects, and the newly relocalized economy (where many goods once produced and imported are now produced locally). Our economy is not geared toward excessive private profits or economic disparity, but is structured instead to maintain the commons and benefit the commonwealth. A centerpiece of this new economy is environmental sustainability, in which ecological impacts always trump economic impacts (the opposite of the situation a decade ago). Again, our economy has shrunk from earlier periods and is no longer based on an irrational metric of constant growth. Sustenance (and sustainability), not profit, is the measure of economic success. Much of this is made possible because value and currency are no longer based on a system of interest and debt (the old financial system has been almost entirely dismantled), but on the commons itself.

INFRASTRUCTURE

The public transit system is expanded significantly, to the extent that a train will take you anywhere in the Lower Mainland quickly. There are very few cars on the streets (many former highways and viaducts have been converted into green spaces), and those that are in use are electric or hydrogen fuel cell. An extensive bike path network makes the city fully accessible to cyclists. Every neighborhood has its own agora, public performance space, and educational center.

COMMONWEALTH

An equitable system of wealth redistribution and radical profit sharing has replaced the former, conventional taxation system. All excess private and corporate profits (above certain, evenly distributed levels) go into the commonwealth to fund infrastructural, social, and cultural programs. "Needs" and "abilities" are carefully assessed so no one falls through the cracks and fails to receive the support of the commonwealth. All bear a responsibility to contribute to the commonwealth as they can, and this is reflected in the system of financial redistribution and "commoning" of shared resources (including profits).

SOCIAL LIFE

Everyone can access free education and health care (or, at least, a system funded in part by reasonable and equitable pay deductions: the commonwealth). Adequate and equitable housing for all is a basic right, and new sustainable neighborhoods, centered on their public spaces and community gardens, are in development everywhere. Direct democratic participation and the practice, exhibition, and performance of the arts are at the core of daily life. Full employment is within reach and those formerly excluded from full participation in society – because of poverty, addiction, mental illness, or whatever – are now welcomed into our inclusive culture, and well on their way to healing. Healing, indeed, is the watchword of a society correcting past social and environmental harms. Corporations, it should be noted, are not considered "people" and have no influence upon social life and programs, other than being vehicles to full employment and contributors to the commonwealth.

The Metabolic Commons; or, From Occupying
to Commoning through Decolonization

> Labour is, first of all, a process between man and
> nature, a process by which man, through his own
> actions, mediates, regulates and controls the
> metabolism between himself and nature.
>
> – KARL MARX
> *Capital*

Karl Marx's mind isn't always the most ecological, and there's much we could say about his colonizer's sense of "controlling" nature, but I've long been quite taken with this metaphor of "metabolism,"[33] and I want, here, to consider the relationship between economics and ecology – between the *how* of making our living on this earth and the *where* of making our living – as a metabolic relationship, and to use this as a basis for an argument in favor of *commoning* as the best "regulator" of this metabolism – instantiating, in fact, a "metabolic commons."

So – metabolism – from the Greek μεταβολη, to change. The *Oxford English Dictionary* gives us the modern biological definition: "the chemical processes that occur within a living organism in order to maintain life."

What I've always marveled at in Marx's use of "metabolism" and his references to "social metabolism" is that – whether Marx went this far or not – it opens the door to seeing the whole economic process as occurring *within* the integral, living bodies of ecosystems, just as it does – in this late moment when human economic activity has come to shape and affect the entire biosphere – pave the way for reading all ecological processes as part and parcel of the contemporary global economic system. The two poles are entirely entwined. David Harvey (commenting on the passage from Marx) puts it this way:

> We cannot transform what's going on around us without transforming ourselves. Conversely, we can't transform ourselves without transforming everything going on around us … This dialectic, of perpetually transforming oneself by transforming the world and vice versa, is fundamental to understanding the evolution of human societies as well as the evolution of nature itself.[34]

Our economies metabolize our ecologies in the process of social metabolism (the building and maintenance of our societies). That the distinctions we tend to draw between the "social" and the "natural" do not really exist shouldn't be too much of a surprise anymore, despite the fact that those driving our very complicated economies do everything they can to mask and disguise this fact (or simply discount it in the name of the bottom line, GDP, or that very reliable election issue – "jobs"). Indeed, corporate and political elites do everything in their power to *oppose* economics to the environment, to make it seem as though we have to choose: it's one or the other, but we can't have both. In some ways they are right: *this particular* economic system and a sustainable and healthy environment may indeed be mutually exclusive – but that's not to say that *another* economic system might not be compatible with ecological balance.

Naomi Klein has recently argued as much: "I think we need to admit that climate change really does demand a profound interrogation of the ideology that currently governs our economy. And that's not bad news, since our current economic model is failing millions of people on multiple fronts."[35] Similarly, in an excellent essay in *The Monthly Review*, John Bellamy Foster – also working from Marx's notion of metabolism – invokes "the unavoidable reality that in a regime in which capital accumulation is the beginning-and-end-all, a sustainable relation to the environment is impossible."[36] Foster continues:

> What was being called for, in the emerging ecological thought of the nineteenth and early twentieth century, was the rational regulation of the human-nature relation. However, "this regulation" of the social-ecological metabolism, Engels observed, "requires something more than knowledge. It requires a complete revolution in our hitherto existing mode of production, and simultaneously a revolution in our whole contemporary social order."

We could put it this way: if an organism burns through its available food supply too rapidly – if its "economy" metabolizes its "environment" too quickly – it soon runs out of external sources of nutrition and, essentially, begins to consume itself. As long as the capitalist economic system had an externality to expand into, it could (fool itself that it could) keep consuming voraciously, and thus keep expanding. Or at least – as soon as it met a limit, which it frequently did, and began to self destructively consume itself, it could find a way past or around that limit (often by "intensifying" the production process, or by technological innovation), and keep expanding; but now that capitalism has reached the limits of the entire planet – now that it has become truly global – there's no where else to go, and any innovative intensification of production will still press against some aspect of the ecological limit. The crises we are living through today – extreme weather caused by a warming climate, soil erosion and deforestation on a vast scale, acidification of the oceans, mass extinctions, debt, foreclosure, bank failures, unemployment, homelessness, etc. – are all signs of a social metabolism gone haywire, of an organism consuming its last reserves.

★

As a means of conceiving of a "complete revolution in our hitherto existing mode of production," what I would like to do here is propose a little imaginative reinvention of Marx's most basic equation about capitalism – the famous C-M-C / M-C-M metamorphoses of commodities and money[37] – by inserting the word (or the concept) "commons" where Marx has "commodity."

In Marx's equation, the series of exchanges, C-M-C, is fairly innocuous, and it isn't capitalism per se. It is based in use value: one begins and ends with something "useful." In a moneyed economy, we all begin with a "commodity" – a product we have produced or a service we can perform; we exchange this commodity or service for money (our paycheck); and then we use the money to purchase useful commodities or services we require. In a capitalist economy, based upon exchange value, this process is more or less reversed (M-C-M). The capitalist begins with money (often as interest-bearing debt); invests that money in products or services (hiring laborers, purchasing means of production); and then through the sale of those products or services, receives money again – plus a profit. Always a profit, a surplus to be reinvested, regardless of what debts may still be outstanding (debt chases debt, like a dog chasing its tail). Constant growth remains the ultimate goal, the constant hypermetabolic movement of capital toward increase.

A capitalist economy begins and ends with money, and its rate of social metabolism is always on the rise, necessarily so, as the whole point of the M-C-M formation is increasing accumulation – money that begets more money.

Now, for clarity of argument as much as anything else, Marx was imagining an individual producer or an individual capitalist entering at C or M. But – in light of our economy's now global reach – what if we imagined the system in its entirety? What *totalities* do we begin and end our process of social metabolism with? Today, our measures for the supposed "health" of the capitalist economy clearly insert and extract the totality of (hypothetical) monetary wealth: what was the *growth* rate of the economy over the course of a year? Did the GDP *rise*? Did the market *grow*? By what percent? Not surprisingly, we're clearly in the realm of the M-C-M rubric. It's also important to note that this totality of money coursing through the economy is *totally abstract* (most of the money doesn't actually, materially "exist") and also, simultaneously, *largely consists of debts owed* somewhere else in the system (every company or individual claiming certain profits *also* carries a sometimes equal, sometimes greater amount of debt).

Along with debt, another thing that is elided here is the question of who owns, and who benefits, from that fiscal totality. How evenly is it distributed? Who owes what to whom, at what rate, and with what expectations of repayment? Who gets what share and why? Who or what suffered to achieve these rates of accumulation? The lie we are sold is, of course, that economic growth is good for us all, and that economic growth always trumps environmental health and sustainability as the ultimate social good. Remember, this is an out-of-control metabolism talking, urging us to keep eating, to have another helping.

But what if we imagined an economic totality that begins and ends with the commons – a new version of the C-M-C equation for a thoroughly globalized system, an economy pushing against its ecological limits? Taken as a whole, all life, all production and reproduction, begins in the commons – at C: intellectually, genetically, we *inherit*, we are *gifted* from past generations, from what already exists. (This is of course what capitalist property relations have long sought to obscure and deny.) All that we depend upon – plants, animals, air, water, soil, knowledge, ideas, technology – come from a common fund. We transform that fund through our social metabolism, acquiring what we need to persist and even prosper. This is at M, which here stands for material production and reproduction – the satisfaction of our needs. Finally – what if the goal of our economy, or our social metabolism, was to return to the commons, to give the gift back – the final position C – so that the commons at the end of our social metabolism was just as healthy and full, *as a totality*, as it was at the beginning of our life process?[38]

This is what I'm calling the metabolic commons. It's the idea that the maintenance, health, and sustainability of the commons should be at the heart of our social metabolism. It's an idea based upon seeing economy and ecology – *how* we make our living and *where* we make our living – as the roots and branches of the same tree. It's an idea based on the complete inseparability of the "social" and the "natural" – an idea that we are simply part of a single large organism that is the biosphere. There only is an atmosphere we can breath, and soil from which all living things can grow, because in the past living things have gone through their cycles of production and reproduction, life and death. At the most primary, metabolic level, we, the totality of living beings, have in fact built the commons upon which we all depend through our collective existences, throughout the course of history, through long cycles of living, dying, and evolving in metabolic exchange with our environments. It is only in the past few centuries that we have had an economy whose mission appears to be to imbalance the metabolic commons and emaciate the future.

★

This essay began as a talk at a conference called The Tragedy of the Market, a phrase that indicates a strange irony: it's not the commons that tragically exceeded its limits of sustainability, as ecologist Garrett Hardin famously proposed, but the market that has done so. I want now to give a fairly straightforward local example of the different "totalities" proposed by the market, on one side, and the commons on the other, as they impact and differently regulate our social metabolism.

A recent *Vancouver Sun* article on the proposed Enbridge Northern Gateway Pipeline noted that "the company and the federal government are pushing for approval, characterizing the project as a national imperative worth $270 billion to the Canadian economy over its lifetime."[39] This is a typical argument for the market, based on a conception of its contribution to the totality of the economy, and leveraged against environmental concerns that could limit economic expansion in any way. As I noted earlier, what's completely missing from the bottom-line figure invoked here ($270 billion) is *who*, exactly, receives what percentage of that total amount, and what environmental and social impacts or consequences will result from such staggering accumulation.

A different picture of the "totality" of a project like the tar sands and its oil pipelines is addressed in another recent article, in the *Vancouver Observer*:

> The Greater Vancouver area is being flooded by several gigantic, uncontrolled and rapidly expanding flows of carbon. All of Vancouverites' efforts to reduce climate emissions in the next decade will be **wiped out one hundred times over** if these local out-of-control carbon flows are allowed to expand as planned.[40]

The point here is imbalance in the metabolic commons, and the totality referenced is atmospheric – the carbon our economy is pumping into the whole biosphere. The uneven development of Big Projects with their highly touted billion-dollar economic contributions, is also at the center of this article. Big Oil and Big Coal, with their planned port expansions and astronomical profit projections, contribute the most to Vancouver's carbon footprint – and do everything they can to avoid paying for the social and environmental damages they cause (while other smaller contributors, like the City of Vancouver itself, *do* pay carbon taxes and endeavor to cut their carbon emissions).

Perhaps the crucial invocation of the sort of "metabolic commons" I am talking about here comes from a recent Tsleil-Waututh Nation press release. Again, the issue is the presence, and proposed expansion, of oil in our local environment. The press release reads, in part:

> "I think it's fair to ask the question 'who speaks for the Burrard Inlet?'" said Chief George, "We take our responsibility for stewardship seriously, but Tsleil-Waututh cannot do it alone. We need the citizens of Metro Vancouver and their local government representatives to get angry and take action over [what] we can only conclude is irresponsible corporate citizenship and ineffectual government regulation."

Chief George concluded: "If you want a glimpse of the future, look at what's happening at present and in our immediate past. Fifteen thousand barrels of oil spilled into the Inlet in the space of less than an hour in 2007. If we continue to allow unregulated industrialization of our backyard, our grandchildren will be lighting fires on the waters of Burrard Inlet."[41]

The notions of "responsibility" and "stewardship" Chief George speaks to here are part and parcel of a traditional First Nations sense of the economic–ecological matrix I'm calling the metabolic commons – the idea that *how* you make your living and *where* you make your living need to be in balance to be sustainable. I turn now to another kind of commons – the future commons – to which Chief George directs my attention.

In some senses, the future is the ultimate commons, as yet unclaimed, unowned, in its entirety (despite leases, titles, and patents that attempt to enclose it). If we are to persist as a society or a civilization or a species, this persistence will by definition depend upon that open future – one to which we will all need access. In a sense, placing present gain before future consequences (upon which capitalism's growth model is based) is already enclosing the future before it arrives. What we require to avoid this real tragedy of the market is exactly what the market system disallows, but which Chief George and the Tsleil-Waututh are calling for: *transgenerational thought and planning*. We need a social metabolism that does not rob us of a common future.

It's in this context of the future commons that I would like to conclude with a few remarks on the Occupy movement. Elsewhere I have written that the real demand or claim the movement is making is the assertion of a right to the future. I see this, in part, in the way the movement has instantly and spontaneously seized hold of public space and – idealistically and without a great deal of planning or forethought – refused to carry the work of an unsustainable system on into the future, even for one more day. It is largely a movement of young people who have their futures ahead of them, and a movement that is built upon sitting down (and standing up), now and without further delay, to fashion a new and better future.

Thus, the Occupy movement remains a movement of potentiality, a movement in a state of potentiality. It's too early – we're only a few months in, after all – to write it off yet. But I'm encouraged by the fact that its main ambit or accomplishment so far has been one of opening possibilities for change and resistance, and for laying a political claim to the very idea of the potential and the future.

So there is a real chance to place the idea of the common – the idea of balanced, shared, and sustainable relations between our economies and our environments – at the heart of the world the Occupy movement might struggle for. The movement, however, has suffered in some ways because of its name, which has sunk in and spread wildly as a meme in these past few months. It has also suffered due to its related failure to adequately address, and find ways of working in solidarity with, existing struggles – particularly those of indigenous communities.

These two issues – the historical implications of the name "Occupy," and the movement's failure to realize full solidarity with indigenous struggles – are obviously interrelated, and have resulted in some calls to "rebrand" the movement with the word "decolonize." First Nations peoples have long had their traditional territories "occupied" – how will this new "occupation" be any different? My hope is that, with the movement still so very much in a state of potential, and with it looking squarely toward a shared or common future, it can indeed respond to this very crucial critique and move forward by decolonizing – and, commoning.

In a recent article, "Decolonizing Together," Harsha Walia writes that

> decolonization is as much a process as a goal. It requires a profound recentring on Indigenous worldviews. Syed Hussan, a Toronto-based activist, states: "Decolonization is a dramatic reimagining of relationships with land, people and the state. Much of this requires study. It requires conversation. It is a practice; it is an unlearning."[42]

Even if the Occupy movement is not able to "rebrand" itself at this point, it still needs to undergo this "profound recentering on Indigenous worldviews" – worldviews, as Walia notes, that "are premised on revolutionary notions of respectful coexistence and stewardship of the land." It also needs to engage in some serious "unlearning," that could, I hope, turn the movement into one of (un)occupying – because this is exactly what a movement toward, and in the name of, a future commons must do. It must release the land we occupy from the choke-hold of colonization, private property relations, and resource extraction, and allow the commons to do the work it is meant to do – regulate the metabolism of our economics and environments so that life may persist into the future.

I think this is also crucial as the meme of occupying proliferates. It's not too hard to imagine "occupying" Wall Street (you foreclose us, we'll foreclose you), but what would it mean to "occupy" the tar sands, or to "occupy" a resource like oil? In the instance of resource industries that are directly damaging the atmospheric commons we all depend upon, what we need, again, is not an occupation, but an unoccupying, an abandoning of destructive and unsustainable industries, a leaving of the oil in the ground. I can think of only one real tried-and-true way of unoccupying, and that's decolonizing, and that's where we need to begin.

Ten Questions (and Answers) on Occupy Vancouver

From its beginning on October 15, 2011, to this day in early January 2012, Occupy Vancouver has prompted many questions about its nature, aims, and practices. I here offer responses to some of the more frequent and wide-ranging of these questions. They are my personal responses, but they also tap into the spirit of the movement, and the experiences and thoughts of many fellow occupiers as I've come to understand them over the months of my interaction and collaborative struggle.

1. IS OCCUPY VANCOUVER ANTI-CAPITALIST?

Occupy Vancouver is a movement for social, economic, and political change – a direct response to current economic and ecological crises. As such its starting point is the realization that the current system is not functioning to the benefit of the majority of people, that the current system is not environmentally or socially sustainable, and that the only real solution is system change. To this extent Occupy Vancouver could be described as "anti-capitalist," but let's first be clear what we mean by "capitalism." Consider these two basic economic propositions:

1. (a) There is nothing inherently wrong with making useful products or providing useful services and selling them in the process of "making a living." (b) There is nothing inherently wrong with purchasing useful products and services that we need with income earned from our own labor.

2. (a) There is, however, something socially destructive about investing in the production of products and services *with the sole purpose of extracting a private profit from investment*. (b) There is also something socially destructive about consuming products and services that fulfill *fabricated desires that extend far beyond basic needs*.

Between these two points stretches the entire history of capitalist evolution – a story of profit making, exploitation, and suffering. Capitalism does not exist at point 1, and Occupy Vancouver is not necessarily "against" an economic model in which people work, make money, and purchase products and services they need. Capitalism, however, is fully realized by point 2, and it is this exploitive and unsustainable system that Occupy Vancouver opposes and seeks to change. Add to this picture capitalism's almost pathological addiction to perpetual growth, its focus on short-term gains over long-term consequences, and the resulting story of environmental destruction this has led to, and it's not exactly easy to accept such a system as "the only alternative." Our work is, in part, to find and articulate an alternative.

2. IS OCCUPY VANCOUVER RUN BY ANARCHISTS?

No – no one runs Occupy Vancouver. Occupy Vancouver is an open and directly democratic movement organized and directed by the consensus of its voluntary participants. Some of these participants would describe themselves as "anarchists," and indeed, the model just described – open, direct democracy and consensus-based decision making – has its roots in anarchist philosophy and practice (as well as in indigenous self-governance). Anarchism is simply democracy without the State – direct democracy in which communities self-organize by providing mutual aid. Anarchism is an idea. It implies social responsibility, self-reliance, and direct community action. It does not mean chaos, disorder, or violence – there is enough of that in the world.

3. HOW DOES SITTING IN A PARK CHANGE ANYTHING?

The Occupy movement begins with a claim upon public space – a claim that, as a society, we need to place the public discussion of our social problems at the center of our definition and experience of "the civic." Instead, what we now have placed at the center of our cities is consumption and entertainment, which is to say, the accumulation of private profit and the distraction/depoliticization of "the public." "Democracy" is largely hidden from view. The Occupy movement seeks to make democracy and its processes visible, inclusive, and unavoidable – as much a part of daily life as eating breakfast. Occupying public space is a way of saying, "We have had enough; the system must change; there are pressing issues we can no longer ignore – let's all get to work and fix this together!"

Sitting in a park might just start to change things if we can successfully embody the idea that our problems won't simply go away – we have to solve them. Sitting in a park might just start to change things if enough of us stop and begin the conversation, publically and openly, about what needs to be done to create a better world.

4. IF YOU WANT TO CHANGE THE WORLD, WHY DON'T YOU JUST VOTE?

Many of us *do* vote – but considering our electoral demographics, many more young people *need* to vote; the Harper government was elected by a relatively small segment of eligible voters, the majority of whom were over forty years old.

But this is only one problem with a representative system. Another is the fact that it is built on the *absence* of its constituents, who (temporary at least) delegate their authority to someone who *re-presents* them in political discussion and debate. Unfortunately, our "representatives" are also indebted to various corporate donors, backers, and lobbyists, and we (the people) have little recourse, between elections, if we are not satisfied with the way they are "representing" us (while corporations and their lobbyists have the ear of elected officials on a daily basis).

It is our frustration with our elected officials' inaction on crucial issues related to the economy, environment, and social programs, as well as frustration with the unresponsiveness of representative democracy as such (which, I will repeat *replaces* an individual's participation with a "representative"), that has alienated many from the electoral system, and which has led Occupy Vancouver into its experiment in direct democracy. The "leaders" have had their chance, and failed. Now, *the people must lead*. After all, that's what "democracy" means.

5. AREN'T THESE AMERICAN PROBLEMS? IT'S NOT AS BAD HERE IN CANADA … YOU'RE JUST COPYING OCCUPY WALL STREET, RIGHT?

Occupy Vancouver stands in solidarity with, and is inspired by, other uprisings worldwide, including the so-called Arab Spring in North Africa and the Middle East, the *Indignado* movement in Spain, anti-austerity protests throughout Europe, and the Occupy Wall Street movement. The reality is that we now live in a global economy, and what happens to the economies of Europe, Asia, or (especially) the United States (75 percent of Canadian exports are to the US)[43] soon happens to us as well.

Canada's economy may not be on as steep a decline as some other countries *yet*, but all the indicators suggest we soon will be. The margin between the richest and the poorest is growing faster in Canada than it is the United States; our personal and public debts are proportionally as alarming; and despite the public perception that there were "no bank bailouts in Canada," there were – again, proportionally comparable to those in the United States.[44]

6. WE DON'T UNDERSTAND WHAT YOU WANT – CAN YOU GIVE US A SPECIFIC DEMAND?

We have essentially one "demand" (though we are reluctant to call it a "demand"): system change. Yes, we know it's a bit presumptuous to ask for everything at once, but the situation is dire and we have to stop "business as usual," reaffirm life, and find new ways – from the ground up – of making our livelihoods.

We are reluctant to speak of "demands" because our one, primary assertion – that the current state of the world demands complete, system-wide change – eliminates or curtails the point of making smaller specific demands of a system that this movement is calling into question.

Nevertheless, we have to find out how to go from where we are now to where we need to be tomorrow. Along the way, we will formulate "calls," outline plans of action, and initiate campaigns for specific social, economic, and political changes – all in open consultation with as many people as we are able to reach out to.

7. IS IT TRUE, AS CANADA'S NATURAL RESOURCES MINISTER, JOE OLIVER, CLAIMS, THAT YOUR ENVIRONMENTAL CONCERNS ARE JUST PART OF A "RADICAL IDEOLOGICAL AGENDA"?[45]

From the perspective of a government determined to maintain a system that benefits a small, privileged elite, sacrificing the natural environment and the very possibility (or possibilities) of a livable tomorrow in the name of short-term profits today, *any* change, *any* challenge to the existing order, is going to seem "radical." But the reality is, the majority of British Columbians oppose the Enbridge Northern Gateway Pipeline.

People who work in offices in Vancouver and enjoy weekends on the water oppose the pipeline, and people who live in Burns Lake and enjoy fly-fishing or mountain biking oppose the pipeline – in short, many people who would not even think of themselves as "environmentalists" are opposed to this project, and other plans to expand tar sands development and oil shipments out of Alberta, risking BC's pristine rivers and wild West Coast waters.

The issue is not jobs – the jobs created by such projects are temporary, and pale in comparison to the jobs *lost* because of the tar sands development. The issue is not profits – the vast billion-dollar "benefits" touted for the entire "Canadian economy," as we all know, are reaped primarily by a few, often foreign-owned, corporations. No, the issue is our future, our children's future, and our grandchildren's future. The issue is the kind of legacy we will leave for tomorrow. Will the world be as livable as today? Will the climate be as tolerable? Will there be jobs – sustainable jobs – tomorrow? These are the "radical" questions we are asking.

8. IS IT TRUE THAT INFIGHTING HAS LED MANY PEOPLE TO LEAVE THE MOVEMENT?

As the saying goes, "this is what democracy looks like." What some might refer to as "infighting," others call vigorous debate. It is only to be expected that people will not always agree with each other. Occupy Vancouver members are all learning how to participate in an open, grass-roots movement for social change. Mistakes will be made – they have been made – and the pressures of the early weeks of the encampment led to many confrontations. It should be noted that these confrontations for the most part did not involve physical violence, that Occupy Vancouver remains committed to non-violence, and that the movement has been working hard on its governance structures and codes of conduct to create an open, fair, and balanced community where all voices can be heard, disagreements accommodated, and yet progress toward collective goals facilitated.

We must concede, however, that obstacles exist. Women, people of color, and LGBT people, for example, have had to contend with two kinds of marginalization: that against which the entire movement struggles, as well as ongoing gender, race, and sexual orientation inequalities to which many (mostly straight, white) men in the movement remain oblivious. The argument sometimes put forward – that issues such as gender and race "distract" from the "main," economic goals of the movement, and are of secondary importance – simply does not hold. We cannot forget that the exploitation we are fighting against uses all means possible to further inequality – including, and often especially, gender, race, and sexual orientation inequality. These are not side issues, but facets of the core issue. The fact that this still needs to be said is perhaps most distressing.

If the movement is to remain strong, its strength, as always, will be directly related to its diversity, mutual respect, and mutual aid. This is what we are trying to live up to.

9. WE HAVEN'T NOTICED MUCH ABOUT YOU GUYS LATELY – ISN'T OCCUPY VANCOUVER OVER NOW?

Don't worry – we haven't gone far. If 2011 was the "year of revolutions," 2012 will be the year of our thoughtful and creative evolution. We're behind the scenes now, organizing, planning, and building the story that will carry all of us forward.

Every social movement needs an initial burst of emotion and indignation to get it going. We had that this past fall. To keep going, we need ideas. We need a story. And we need relationships. This part takes a bit of time.

At Occupy Vancouver, since being evicted on November 21, we have been resting up and assessing what we have accomplished – really, the beginning we have made. We've been talking, reading, writing, filming, and planning for the future. We are working hard within our committees, and on our relationships with each other and with other organizations. We are gearing up for the work ahead – the work of social transformation that a time of economic, ecological, and political crisis demands.

10. HOW ARE YOU GOING TO GET THE 99% ON YOUR SIDE IF YOU KEEP DISRUPTING AND INCONVENIENCING THEM?

We live in a world of "disruptions" and "inconveniences." This is what mass social life is like in the twenty-first century. Change occurs in our world every day, whether we actively seek it out or not; when we do actively engage in the process of social change, there will indeed be things people find disruptive and inconvenient.

One problem we are trying to address in this movement is the fact that an economy built on "conveniences" (oil and gas for our cars, high-tech materials mined all over the world, global trade, etc.) is not a sustainable economy. Some of the changes we need to make will be achieved through replacing older, carbon-heavy industries with new, carbon-neutral industries (especially in the energy sector). But the reality is that we are all going to have to find ways to reshape our lives that will at first seem disruptive and inconvenient. Anything worth struggling for will cause some amount of pain.

We should be angry. But let's remember *what* we should be angry at: a system of chronic inequality and environmental destruction – a system that sacrifices a sustainable tomorrow for a convenient today – this is something that should outrage us all.

Together, the whole 99% can participate in and ease the burden of a changing world and a new definition of daily life. This is, in fact, the main difference between today's "conveniences" and tomorrow's sustainability: truly, we do not equally share the burden of today's disruptions, but we can and must share the burden of tomorrow's, and we will find that the shared burden will not weigh as heavily once the load is distributed more equitably.

This question is perhaps the greatest challenge facing Occupy Vancouver and the whole global Occupy movement. We have a story to tell, a new world to outline. But more importantly, we are ready to listen, if you are ready to take that adventurous step into the imagination, and join us in a conversation about what sort of world we all might like to share. There is no one way to organize a society. Let's see what we can come up with.

A Show of Hands:

Art and Revolution in Public Space

Progressive social movements do not simply
produce statistics and narratives of oppression;
rather, the best ones do what poetry always
does: transport us to another place, compel us
to re-live horrors and, more importantly,
enable us to imagine a new society.

— ROBIN KELLEY
Freedom Dreams

I have two dialectics on my mind – one, something of a false
dialectic, to which I think I know the solution, and another which
– necessarily – remains an unresolved tension. The first, false
dialectic is the old, new, constantly renewed tension between the
private and the public. That's the one I think I know the solution
to, or at least which I'm willing to *propose* a resolution to, and I'll
get to that in just a bit. The other is the tension formed between art
and revolution, which continues to puzzle and propel my work,
both as a poet and as an activist. The second dialectic, I will also
suggest, is played out on the ground of the first. I'll begin with the
public/private diad then, before turning to art and revolution.

★

What happens when we share public space, when we meet randomly in public? If we are lucky – if we are not too busy, too rushed, too turned in on our "own shit" – we regard each other. At some level, we "see" each other, and recognize each other – as human. Maybe "people watching" is judgmental ("just look at this guy … who'd dress like that?"). But it can also shift, unpredictably, instantly, as we loiter in some public space, into recognition of the otherness of the other, the undeniable humanness of the other *outside of ourselves*, the legitimacy of the other and our responsibility to the other (we exchange a smile or nod; a knowing look, having both just observed the same absurd thing; we see that we are both human, both unavoidably *here*, almost nakedly so, with no other excuse than having stepped into the same, shared space for a moment). We find each other in public. We realize our multiplicity in public. The eyes have it. The face. We are all *fundamentally* in this together. The planet's spinning somewhere uncertain, and here we are together. Now what?

It is clear that – as far as the State is concerned – certain activities are permissible in public space, certain others are not. Commercial activities, "public" celebrations of sporting events, civic holidays, and holiday traditions – these are, by and large, allowable. Camping overnight to be first in line for a sale: okay. Camping overnight to assert democratic and charter rights … not so much.

The problem, at least in part, is this: what we think of as "public" space is, paradoxically, entirely privatized. Our "public" spaces are owned – either by private enterprises that provide them via development agreements with the city in question, or they are "owned" by the city in question, which exerts the right to determine the terms and extent of their use. "Public" spaces have security cameras and guards who monitor and intervene. "Public" spaces typically close at certain times of the day, and categorically limit and exclude certain uses. "Public" spaces serve private, capital-accumulating interests ("Come enjoy the facilities before returning to work or shopping"). What we are missing, now, is a truly public space, a free, relatively unadministered space that could be a common space – one neither publically nor privately owned, but truly and to the letter *belonging to the commons*.

This "belonging" is not the same as "owning." A common space "belongs" to the commons the way two arms and two legs "belong" to the morphology of a human being. It's a matter of the "properties" of an organic being, rather than the "property" owned by a legal entity.

Consider this passage from Justice Anne MacKenzie's decision to evict Occupy Vancouver from the Vancouver Art Gallery lawn in November 2011: "the City says it would suffer irreparable harm if the injunction were not granted. Specifically, the public would suffer irreparable harm in terms of access to, and use of, public space."[46]

It is difficult not to stumble over the paradox here: "access" is to be protected by an injunction debarring a certain form of access. The City of Vancouver here places itself in the position of "the public" (as its "representative"), and argues that the use being made of this particular "public" space by Occupy Vancouver causes "irreparable harm" to other potential uses of the same space. First, the City is asserting its exclusive rights to decide what uses of "public" space are legitimate and what uses are not (thus acting as a private owner of the space). Second, the City is asserting that one use of public space is exclusive of other potential uses of such space (thereby employing a scarcity model – *there's not enough!* – again, thinking exclusively in the terms of private and single ownership).

The word "thinking" is important here: privatization has so colonized space and *thought* that the proposal of something actually common is difficult to imagine, almost impossible to conceive of. This may be why the Occupy movement is in fact (somewhat inappropriately) called the *Occupy* movement: it was difficult to conceive of a relation to space outside of its *occupation* – its seizure, control, claiming, or reclaiming – outside the dynamics of its exclusive use. However, the word *unsettles* (and this may, ultimately, be its saving grace) a history of colonization and *settlement* through which aboriginal and many other marginalized groups have long had their lands "occupied"; they might rightly ask how is this new occupation going to solve anything? Really, what has been undertaken by the Occupy movement is an *un*-occupation, an attempt to take back "occupied" space from the State/corporation – to liberate space from the dynamics of ownership and capital. It is a dream of a once and future commons.

Without getting into a discussion about whether Occupy Vancouver was willing to "share" the VAG lawn or not (it was), the point I take from all this is that what we think we mean by "public space" (free and open to all – the opposite of private property) doesn't actually exist in our society – because even the supposedly "public" is policed and regulated by its "owner," a governmental body supposedly representing the "public" at large, but ultimately acting in a proprietary fashion, much as any private property owner would, or in the interests of certain private stakeholders and "investors."

Indeed, what we often see on the VAG lawn are public/private partnerships, such as corporate-sponsored events. (Note the CIBC LunarFest encamped outside the art gallery in the first week of February, charging for food where Occupy Vancouver provided free food, and seemingly being allowed to use heating sources indiscriminately inside its tents, where Occupy Vancouver was removed for supposed "fire hazards.")

Common land, as a general term for land that is not conceived of as owned or even *ownable* (whether privately or publically), was the basis of many societies the world over for much of human existence. The commons was a space – it was *most* space in fact – upon which we relied to find what we needed to survive. Its "enclosure," to take the example of English history (the despoilment of the Americas by European colonial powers is another ripe example), was part and parcel of separating the peasantry (or indigenous peoples) from their independent sustenance-based economy and making them available for wage labor, and their land available for commodity crops and the private accumulation of wealth.

To cut to the chase, the private/public diad has already been dissolved – everything is private, and no truly public space or public sphere exists anymore; to resolve the apparent dialectic of private versus public – which is in fact to propose a new dialectical tension, a new opposition to the now universal rule of the private – we need to propose common space.

The point is that a "commons" is a space a population uses for satisfying its social needs; it is a space of collective independence – no one owns it, but ideally, all have use of it. It is in fact *constituted* by those users and uses – a *constituent* space. The Occupy movement has essentially been asserting a right to a new kind of commons – a political commons upon which all are invited to enter into the ongoing democratic process of governing ourselves.

★

The question of art and revolution has hovered around Occupy Vancouver, perhaps to an extent not seen in other urban occupations, in part simply because *this* occupation was on the lawn of its city's art gallery, and because *this* city's space most clearly identified with political demonstration is, in fact, an art gallery lawn (rather than, say, a central square in front of a government building or an urban park deep in a city's financial district). The idea was in fact proposed, several times, by several different individuals, to declare the occupation a "site-specific" or "performance" work, or an "installation." Essentially, this would have been done to "get the city off the occupation's back," rather than to say anything specific about art or revolution or the relationship between art and revolution.

But it does raise some interesting questions: why is it permissible to place artwork in "public" spaces, but not protest camps? Is art really that safe? That connected to the State's sense of its self-valorization as "cultural patron"? Considering what I've said already about public space being simply a variant of private space, the answer to the latter question has to be "yes" – art is allowed in public because the State or other private/public partnerships see it as an attractive ornament to its unremittingly commercial surface.

Lunacharsky once wrote that "if revolution can give art its soul, then art can give revolution its mouthpiece."[47] But the two remain largely uncomfortable bedfellows. To rebrand the occupation of the VAG lawn an "aesthetic" project would court Benjamin's famous dictum: "All efforts to render politics aesthetic culminate in one thing: war."[48]

Following Gerald Raunig, I would eschew "models of totally diffusing and confusing art and revolution," reading them instead as "neighboring zones ... in which transitions, overlaps and concatenations of art and revolution become possible for a limited time, but without synthesis and identification."[49] There is no tidy way to reconcile or unite art and revolution, the VAG and Occupy Vancouver: they necessarily remain "neighboring zones." But such "neighboring" is of interest because it is an active space, a dynamic borderland, a relationality through which energies pass back and forth, a space in which tensions remain productive, and thus a space in which change occurs.

The events at Occupy Vancouver had the VAG's neoclassical façade, and the large banner for the *Shore, Forest and Beyond* exhibition as their constant backdrop. Maybe a few activists wandered inside. Certainly patrons of the gallery wandered past the occupation, wondering what it was all about as they entered the building.

When it comes to their publicness – their being in supposedly public space – an interesting thing about both art and revolution is revealed in their neighborliness. With art, its content begins to matter more when it is encountered in public, while with activism, its form matters more than its content. Consider media artist Kota Ezawa's *Hand Vote* in this regard.[50]

As a more or less representational work, we are immediately drawn to the content of the image – its representation of a group of people with their hands raised, in the act of voting. Are they a group of political representatives? It's possible – but there's a feeling more of the classroom here, or the town hall. It could even be a parents' advisory committee – we don't know. What we do come away with is a sense of the moment of democratic action – the crucial moment when, as participants and constituents, we see each other's hands and understand each other's positions. The show of hands in a public space is the oldest and most direct form of democracy – the self-management of the commons – how do we organize what we share, so we can go on sharing it? It's worth noting that the use of hand signals has been one of the distinctive aspects of the Occupy movement – especially the consensus-expressing "sparkle fingers." (There are countless photographs of occupiers with their hands in their air.) At this moment in time, hands publically raised in the process of direct democratic decision making have new, more revolutionary meaning. It's an icon of this historical moment.

Here's my point: the *form* of the hand vote, and its connection to direct democratic process – especially in reoccupied "public" space – is suddenly a revolutionary form. As a *representation* in Kota's image, it is revolutionary *content*. But the "overlap" and "concatenation" between the "neighboring zones" of art and revolution here (and form and content, for that matter) reveals the really interesting complexity in this image: it is *representational* (safe, recognizable as art, allowable in public) of the *non-representational*, directly democratic moment (unsafe; not art, but protest; not allowed in privately controlled "public" space).

This tension – unresolvable – between representation in art and representation in politics – lies at the heart of the art and revolution matrix, and is only really revealed by the two poles being able to "neighbor" each other in "public," as they do here in Kota's *Hand Vote* – and as they did for thirty-eight days during the occupation of the VAG lawn. At the same time, it reveals the very problem of the *privacy* of the public. Indeed, VAG's "offsite" space is, much like Occupy Wall Street's now famous Liberty (Zuccotti) Park, a very *private* public space – a portion of private space provided for "public use" as part of the package "sold" to the City by the developers of the Shangri-La complex. Thus it is significant that what we find ourselves doing now, at this historical juncture, in these complicated spaces, is the seemingly simply and innocuous act of showing our hands – and our faces – to each other in as direct and unmediated a fashion as possible. We are revealing ourselves to each other, and revealing our willingness to meet each other as equals. In this way, we work toward a new consensus on a reoccupied commons.

Casserole

We were what the
Evenings were for –
Gigantic waves of
Crashing sound
Passing interiors
Lit like paintings
From the renaissance –

So much spring you
Could bang the pots
And pans of each
Evening – smile at
Every stranger you
Know also wanted a
Totally different world –

Somewhere we'd write
Pop songs about the
Changes we were making
And not feel the slightest bit
Disingenuous – even when
It played on a car radio
Its windows wound down in the rain

From State Shift to "Shift State":

Resistance to Civil Government 2012

As spring gives way to summer, much of the energy that has been fueling the Occupy movement in Canada is now manifesting itself in demonstrations in solidarity with the Quebec student movement and the Montreal "casseroles" (spontaneous night-time pot banging marches – a wordless defiance of the new anti-protesting law, Bill 78). As the movement continues to unfold and morph, we need to keep in mind the reasons behind its tactics, and the ever-growing need for more discussion, debate, and the generation of movement ideas and goals.

Ultimately, what we need to be doing is building solidarity, building a broad-based movement in which more and more people wish to and can participate (whether their concern is mounting student debt, climate change, or the corrupt influence of money in politics). We need to get back to what brought us to activism in the first place: the realization that there is a great deal of injustice in the world, and that the world can and must be changed – by our direct participation and actions. We can "casserole" all we want – but until we have something *to put in the pot*, as it were, we may not be able to build a large enough movement.

To do this, to bring numbers together, above all, we need a *story*, a *vision*, an *idea*. We need something for people to gather around, participate in, join and support – not just something to reject, oppose, or protest *against*.

In other words, *what are we for*? I think we all have to ask ourselves this question. We have to meet and discuss our ideas and visions together, and find our common ground. And then we have to build that story/vision/idea, and share it far and wide. I can only begin to touch on some of this complexity here – by reminding of the urgency of the present situation, and the paths we have to take to find our way to real, meaningful change.

1. STATE SHIFT

I begin with two seemingly unrelated things: one, a recent report in the journal *Nature*; the other, the passing, more or less as I write this, of the Harper government's omnibus Bill C-38. Both are more than a little depressing, but both also point in directions that could help us get out of our current mess and past these, let's call them "threshold," moments.

The *Nature* article, "Approaching a State Shift in Earth's Biosphere," is authored by some twenty scientists from a broad range of related fields. The argument goes something like this: just as local ecosystems are known to shift abruptly from one state to another when forced over certain thresholds, it is becoming increasingly apparent that the entire planetary biosphere could also be forced into a more or less sudden state shift. There is mounting evidence that we are within ten to fifteen years of such a tipping point. The report states:

> Although the ultimate effects of changing biodiver-
> sity and species compositions are still unknown, if
> critical thresholds of diminishing returns in ecosys-
> tem services were reached over large areas and at the
> same time global demands increased … widespread
> social unrest, economic instability and loss of human
> life could result.[51]

The factors leading to potential state shift include "human population growth with attendant resource consumption, habitat transformation and fragmentation, energy production and consumption, and climate change."

If we are paying any attention at all, this story is becoming ever more familiar; studies like this latest one in *Nature* simply add detail to the picture through solid research. Plant and animal species are now disappearing at rates on par with the extinction of the dinosaurs. Human-generated climate change is reaching a point beyond which the planet will not be able to recover. This is not an opinion or theory anymore. It's the more or less unanimous position of the entire scientific community, based on an ever-increasing body of research. We need to start thinking seriously about how we are going to live in a drastically changed and changing world.

2. THE FROZEN STATE

Now, consider the *Nature* report alongside the other piece of news: the passage of Bill C-38. While the new legislation attacks the Canadian social safety net from almost every angle with a host of austerity measures, it arguably does the *most* damage to the environment, by watering down or eliminating much of Canada's environmental protection laws and generally speeding up, centralizing, and removing oversight mechanisms for the approval of large resource-based development projects (pipelines, mines, tar sands).

That reports like the one published in *Nature* – as well as the growing chorus of other concerned voices from the scientific community – do not appear to phase the Harper government is no real surprise. This is a government that has been very upfront about its "disagreement" with science – which more or less amounts to "disagreeing" that today is in fact Friday, or that the sun will in fact rise again on Saturday.

Nevertheless, the shortsightedness of this government – and other governments that everywhere are failing to heed the dire warnings of the scientific community – continues to baffle, defying both logic and empathy. How is such shortsightedness possible? How, when it's clear that we need to rapidly wean ourselves from fossil fuels, can a government stake all its plans and priorities on expanding fossil-fuel production and dependence?

Someday I would like to write a book about the demented psychology of State government that helps explain this problem. It must have something to do with the way modern electoral politics has become inseparable from crass calculations of the metric needed to win an election, which largely involves rallying a party's base and completely ignoring the rest of the electorate deemed unnecessary for winning the election. The complete absorption of electoral politics in "winning the next election" is comparable to the absorption of the market in the next quarter's (or even next day's) performance. As David Graeber argues in *Debt: The First 5,000 Years*, "capitalism seems to be uniquely incapable of conceiving of its own eternity."[52] For both State governments and capitalism, the stakes are high, you are only as good as your last win, and tomorrow may very well bring about your downfall. So walk the tightrope as long and far as you can.

Handy, when the gambler's mentality rules our world. Add to this the fact that privilege, quite simply, *always defends and justifies itself*, just as it always feels the effects of conditions that might *force it to change* long after the "less privileged" rest of us feel the same, and we are a long way toward understanding why our governments don't change when it's crystal clear that change is upon us, whether we want it or not. There's also the whole problem of corporate influence; for the most part, our governments do what their biggest donors and class allies want them to do. But let's save that discussion for another day.

3. SHIFT STATE

I think a government's inability to act in the best interest of future society is equal to, and perhaps the direct result of, its inability to care for the commons – to think beyond its "base," and beyond its ability to "get away with" an agenda that serves only a small elite. The language of the commons that hovers around the political sphere – "house of commons," "commonwealth" – registers as largely ironic. There is nothing much common about our political system now: it is in the service of capital accumulation and the few who benefit the most from this process, and what we're told is: *be happy with the few crumbs falling from the table.*

The Harper government's inability to heed the warnings of science, combined with (and embodied in!) the passage of destructive legislation like Bill C-38, tells us something about what our strategy needs to be now. The various online petitions and social media campaigns aimed at stopping the legislation, though well intentioned and organized, had little hope in light of Harper's majority government. Sadly, there's not much that can be done, through the established political channels, between now and the next election.

But that just means we have to organize *outside* of the established channels.

If governments like Harper's won't respond to the coming "state shift," then we have to *shift the State* – by shifting outside the State's institutional structures. This is exactly what has been happening this past year, first with the Occupy movement, and now with the Quebec solidarity "casseroles" across the country. What we need is movement building: a movement grounded in the commons – in *care for* the commons, which is simultaneously care for the future that we share. This is democracy as stewardship of the commons, by the commons, for the commons. We need a movement against the damage in which legislation like Bill C-38 is complicit – damage to the natural environment and the commons, damage to First Nations' territories and traditional ways of life, damage to citizens' rights and freedoms, damage to workers' opportunities and well-being. We need a movement that – when the next election does come around – will allow us to genuinely use the electoral system to reverse some of the damage currently being done, and in turn reform that electoral system so the sorts of abuses we are now suffering will not be possible in the future.

This is where I would begin to fashion a story, vision, and idea that could become the ground and basis of value in this movement: the commons. The commons as that which we all share in the broadest sense: civil society itself, all the "natural resources" life consists of and depends upon, all the cultural ideas and practices that are our shared inheritance as human beings. We are a small community when it comes down to it – every human being on the planet, a recent issue of *National Geographic* noted, could stand together for a "family photograph," taking up no more space than that of greater Los Angeles.[53] And our current lives and our potential futures depend upon what we have in common – the air, earth, water, all the stories and knowledge and cultural practices accumulated over the generations – than anything one person or group can claim to "own."

For now, we need the streets, and we need pots and pans. But even this must be little more than a prelude and means to deeper organization. We cannot simply hope to increase the numbers of willing casserole participants week by week, until we somehow overwhelm the government. We, too, will run up against the metric of our "base," or at least fall into the calculus Graeber warns against: "any system that reduces the world to numbers can only be held in place by weapons."[54] That's the State's game. It can't be ours.

What we need to do is start to find ways to enact and protect real commons now. We need education (which is exactly where the whole Red Square movement began, remember); we need information; we need street teams and forums, discussions, and ideas – in our neighborhood communities and everywhere else. We need to collectively develop detailed pictures of a viable world strikingly different from the one the likes of Harper serves – and we need to get these pictures into as many hands as possible, by as many means as possible. We need orators, poets, artists, musicians, philosophers, activists, and organizers. We need to reach out to everyone everywhere in ways the State can't – or won't.

In other words, we need to get even deeper into the *grass* and its *roots*. So go ahead and bang your pots and pans. But get ready to talk, too, and to organize, when the din dies down.

PART 3

LETTER FROM ROME

The philosophers have only *interpreted* the
world in various ways; the point, however, is
to *change* it.

– KARL MARX
"Theses on Feuerbach"

Dear Commoners,

I address these comments on politics and change to everyone and
anyone. A democracy is management of the commons, by the
commons, for the commons. It's you – us – that I/we need to talk
to. Together and alone.

I am a poet drawn to Rome, as poets have been for centuries.
Because poets are time mechanics, angels of history, and here in
Rome we can see (so it seems) all history spread out before us,
revealed layer by layer down to the mysterious base. I wander and
watch in the galleries and ruins. At the Protestant Cemetery I
stand first by Shelley's, then by Keats's grave.

Shelley's epitaph, taken from *The Tempest* – "Nothing of him
that doth fade, / But doth suffer a sea-change / Into something rich
and strange" – counterbalances Keats's nameless "Here lies one
whose name was writ in water." Change as mysterious power of
metamorphosis or change as our fleet-footed, swiftly approaching
fate – transformer or eraser – we know we cannot resist it, only find
ways to navigate its storms and bursts.

Everywhere we turn in Keats's life, the temporalities of the fleeting and the eternal mix and give off sparks. From the figures on his
"Grecian Urn," frozen forever in a moment of youthful frenzy, to
his name writ imperceptibly in water, through his fears that he may
die before his pen has gleaned his teeming brain (well-founded
fears, it turned out), Keats wrote under the pressure of an intense
awareness of swift and inevitable and irreversible change.

For myself, I go out under the Roman sun. Crowds seethe all
around. I am attracted to the birds – first pigeons, and now as the
weather warms, swallows – which soar around and roost in the

Pantheon's eroded façade. I watched for several days before I caught sight of one flying inside the dome. It was inevitable. I wanted to remember its brevity inside that timeless cosmic sphere.

I have been obsessed about the Occupy movement for months now, and this is a brief retreat. I need to think – what is the difference between those changes that seem to *befall* us, and those changes we might seek to "make"? What does it mean, to say, "This changes everything"? What does it mean to say, "Another world is possible"? What does it mean to declare a movement *in the name of change*? How is change something we can – certainly not *control* – but – have a *say* in? I'm off among the stones to find out.

★

April 18

We did not begin in Rome; we were in Paris first, tracking the traces of the various revolutions – places where barricades had once stood, where kings and queens had been beheaded, where palaces had burned to the ground. In Rome, the rain fell as we drove into the city through the Porta San Paolo, past the Pyramid of Cestius, Keats and Shelley lying in their graves just beyond – along the side of the Circo Massimo and around the Campidoglio, and at last into the warren of streets where the Pantheon lay, deep in its cobbled nest.

I have come to Rome because it is the Eternal City – it seemed that a supposedly *changeless* place would be the right place to think about change. If Rome is "a city destined to endure as long as the human race survives,"[1] it's here we might best ponder the ubiquitous dialectic of permanence and mutability, as well as the uncertainties of the path we are now upon.

So we have set up residence beside the Pantheon – one of the oldest, continually-in-use buildings in the world, and the best-preserved ruin of Imperial Rome. Up four flights of worn marble stairs, I look out at the east side of the massive temple through my open window. Leaning back in my chair, I can see the portico, its gigantic granite pillars (quarried in Egypt, or possibly repurposed from an Egyptian temple), and the small square and fountain beyond.

Where our apartment sits – on the Via della Minerva – the Saepta Julia once stood. So called after its reconstruction by Julius Caesar, it was an ancient voting precinct – this whole area of Rome, the Campus Martius, had long been used for the Roman people to assemble to vote in consuls and other magistrates. The emperors soon had little interest in voting, as Republic gave way to Empire, so games began to be held where a participatory democracy was once practiced. Nero, it's said, flooded the Saepta and held mock naval battles there – for entertainment.

I have come here to think about democracy and change, about the revolutionary tradition's fascination with republican Rome (in 1794 Saint-Just proclaimed, "The world has been empty since the Romans, their memory is now our only prophecy of freedom"),[2] and about the problem of republics fading slowly into empires (as well as the possibility, if any, of empires suddenly giving way to republics). Rome has long been the touchstone for both imperial ambition and radical politics. This is the struggle today – will we give ourselves over once and for all to the empire of global capital, or will we finally institute real democracy now (*¡Democracia Real YA!*),[3] and act collectively in all our best interests, choosing our common wealth over private interest?

★

April 19

The square in front of the Pantheon is smaller, and many feet higher, than it was in antiquity – giving the Pantheon the appearance of having sunk slightly into the ground. The building itself has suffered much in its almost two thousand years. Byzantine Emperor Constans II took its gilded bronze roof tiles in 663, having another use for them (despite the building's having been consecrated a Christian church in 609). Passages were cut through pillars near its southern apse. A bell tower was added over the center façade in the thirteenth century (it is gone now), and in the early seventeenth-century twin towers were added at the ends of the intermediate block (also gone – for a time referred to as its "donkey's ears"). Shops and booths were built between the portico's columns (you can still see slots cut in the pillars where they were anchored). The eastern part of the porch itself collapsed, but was restored under Popes Urban VIII and Alexander VII in the seventeenth century; Urban VIII also removed two hundred tons of bronze from the support system of the porch – to forge cannons. There is graffiti – some by children, and some by popes.

Much of the exterior of the Pantheon is scored, scoured, and gouged – like someone has tried very hard to scrape all culture and beauty from its crumbling rock core. The pillars of its portico are cracked and chipped in some places, and only a few of their capitals remain close to whole – but they are magnificent just the same – as though freshly formed out of a dusky gelato. The exterior of the rotunda looks like many another squat medieval tower that has withstood countless assaults over the centuries. It is now home to pigeon and swallow nests, and weeds sprout from cracks and gaps. Only one thing retains the air of perfection, the air of being untouched by time: the glory of the interior dome and its oculus. As unchanged as the heavens it was meant to represent.

But the heavens, we know, are not unchanging. Stars and galaxies have their births and distant deaths, their expenditure of energy and inevitable collapse. All Rome's seeming eternity, too, is mere perception. We occupy a small observation point in time, watching it glow. Cafés and stores we knew when we were here five years ago are gone, new ones cut into the sides of aging buildings. Rome is a few remnants, like the Pantheon, of its republican and imperial past, amid a hodgepodge of medieval structures and streets built from the decaying or deconstructed ancient city – *spoglie* – "spoils," they were called. "Medieval Rome did not merely rise on the site of ancient Rome," historian Robert Hughes observes, "it was, quite literally, made from its remains."[4] On top of this is a renaissance veneer of palaces and squares, with a few "modern" additions and adjustments. Free WiFi hotspots are provided by the State and marked with small signs, though they do not work very well. Rome might as well be made of the water that flows through its aging pipes and aqueducts, to burble forth from its countless fountains. All that's solid floods and flows, and we never step in the same Rome twice.

★

April 20

History is the subject of a structure whose
site is not homogenous, empty time, but time
filled by the presence of the now [*Jetztzeit*].
Thus, to Robespierre ancient Rome was a
past charged with the time of the now which
he blasted out of the continuum of history.
The French Revolution viewed itself as Rome
incarnate. It evoked ancient Rome the way
fashion evokes the costumes of the past.

– WALTER BENJAMIN
"Theses on the Philosophy of History"

Because human culture is cumulative – because culture is our
major adaptation as a species, allowing us to pass information
along *outside of our genes*, and because we accumulate more and
more cultural information to pass on – we are forever citing back
along the record we carry within culture for past analogues to help
explain and order new experiences of the now. The past, forever,
leaps into the present as useful comparison points present themselves to our inquisitive and acquisitive minds (or as old night-
mares – or old hopes for release and salvation – present themselves
again). So for French revolutionaries and for reformers of all
stripes in the eighteenth century – after more than a millennium
of largely autocratic, monarchial rule – the ancient Roman
Republic was what came leaping like a tiger from the literary
tradition. It was a sign beckoning a new, though very old, direction.
The common people were once again about to step onto the stage
of history, and make their hopes and desires *public*.

A democracy is what we might take to be our shared work. *Res publica* – a public thing – to be held in common, all of us responsible for its course and outcome. Rousseau (one of those key, eighteenth-century revivers of ancient Rome): "In the republics and even in the monarchies of the ancient world, the people never had representatives ... the moment a people adopts representatives it is no longer free; it no longer exists."[5]

The "people," present and actively participating in history – this is what France called back to Rome for, and which, in some way shape or form, I can't help feeling we need to call back for again, since the common cause is lost once more to the "representatives," that small exclusive percent who control and largely benefit from the course of human affairs, as they direct it toward their, and their allies', whims. It seems we've given democracy little thought in the past two hundred years, satisfied that we've settled all of that. Really, we just swept it under the carpet of private property rights and capitalist accumulation. Out of sight, out of mind.

Of ancient Greece and Rome, Hannah Arendt notes that

> freedom was understood as being manifest in cer-
> tain ... human activities ... [that] could appear and
> be real only when others saw them, judged them,
> remembered them. The life of a free man needed the
> presence of others. Freedom itself needed therefore
> a place where people could come together – the
> agora, the market-place, or the *polis*, the political
> space proper ... [T]he actual content of freedom
> [was] participation in public affairs.[6]

The past leaping into the present – to announce the entrance of the common people into history once again – to fill the squares of cities (whether forum or agora, Puerta del Sol or Zuccotti Park), again making a public thing of our politics – this is what the Occupy movement has come to announce – even here in Rome, the one city where, on October 15, 2011, the day the world's cities were occupied, the "non-violent" movement unfolded with considerable "violence."

★

April 21

What does not change … is the persistence of change.

Tradition has it that Rome was founded 2,765 years ago today. In the Capitoline Museums, we stare at the foundations of the sixth century, its long-demolished Temple of Jupiter. A few floors away, I gaze into the face of the *Dying Gaul*, who seems only marginally concerned about his fate, as his marble brow tilts toward the earth he will soon become a part of. In the netting above the courtyard of the Palazzo Nuovo – a dead bird, its wings partly spread, hangs in the air over marble nymphs, gods, and heroes. As if frozen there in midflight. And I recall, on my way to the museum, a disheveled man playing an accordion outside the Banca Di Roma.

It's said that on April 21 the emperor would arrive at the Pantheon and – at a certain hour (from what I've observed, around midday) – the giant bronze doors would be thrown open, and he would step dramatically into a natural spotlight, the beam from the oculus filling the entranceway perfectly. Art historian William MacDonald explains:

> The imperial system claimed, if not perfection, success and permanence. Order and the system were synonymous, and the most orderly of geometric, and therefore of architectural, shapes is the circle. It is without corners and seams, and has no beginning and no end. It stands for continuity … In a very real sense, the Pantheon rotunda is a metaphor in architecture for the ecumenical pretensions of the Roman Empire.[7]

Every stay against impermanence is simply some other form of the temporary. Emperors and popes may etch their names in stone, but this is just a slower-to-fade form of the water in which the rest of us write our names. Exiting the Pantheon early this morning, a worker was guiding a large red polishing machine across the floor – ahead of the arrival of the hordes of tourists who will come to take their photographs (which will fade one day, or get deleted from a hard drive). I wonder what his name is, or what he makes of his own reflection in the polished marble floor.

★

April 22

Livy, early in his first-century *History of Rome*, tells the story of an "old man" who "presented himself in the Forum."[8] Emaciated by hunger and his clothes torn and dirty, a crowd gathered to hear his story. His crops destroyed while he was in military service, debt and accumulating interest did the rest as he struggled, and failed, to recover from his losses.

Reading this, and about the "internal discord of the ever-increasing bitterness between the ruling class and the masses," the "chief cause" of which "was the plight of the unfortunates who were 'bound over' to their creditors for debt," I couldn't help thinking of the recent story from Greece, where the aging pensioner Dimitris Christoulas, despairing of his financial struggle amid government austerity measures, took his life, so as not to be a burden to his children, in front of the Greek parliament on Syntagma Square, April 4, 2012.

"So I won't leave
debts for my children"

Some will or
whatever fatality
out of Greek drama
starved of art
and thinking for
seventy-seven years

"You can't go on
robbing the young
of their futures"

Arms will rise
and they won't always
point guns at
their own heads

Pensioner, pharmakon,
what physic breaks
out of minds
winged with light
where nobody notices?

"This government has
annihilated all traces
of my survival"

So this end has come
before resorting to
garbage for food
behind a tree
on Syntagma Square

I'm wondering now
what sort of tree
carves no governments
hearts at its core

What was true of Livy's Rome is true again today: the financial excesses of a tiny elite are being paid for by a struggling majority. "Money-lenders had used all their influence and employed every device to produce a situation which was ... unfavorable to the commons," Livy tells us – thus "the commons as a whole were sunk in debt, and the situation could not be remedied without general relief ... Political decisions, however, always have been, and always will be, influenced for ill by party spirit and concern for property."[9]

When the political system does not allow space in public consciousness for the suffering of certain classes, when certain people become entirely invisible, the validity and viability of the entire social structure is called into question. How can such a system endure?

The question of durability – of the stability of the form of government – seems to inevitably enter political debates. What system will provide the greatest stability over the greatest period of time? Rousseau famously found democracy's very fragility (in terms of its mutability) worth defending:

> There is no government so liable to civil war and internecine strife as is democracy or popular government, for there is none which has so powerful and constant a tendency to change to another form or which demands so much vigilance and courage to maintain it unchanged.[10]

The idea of one form of government "changing to another" recalls the classical theory of the cyclical nature of political revolution – the inevitability (this in Aristotle and Polybius) of monarchy transforming into oligarchy transforming into democracy transforming into monarchy again and so on. An idea struck upon in the classical world, and resurrected as the idea of Rome was revived in the eighteenth century, is that of the "perfectly mixed and balanced constitution," Polybius's "combination of all three varieties" – kingship (president), aristocracy (senate), and democracy (commons) – a form named "republican" (that "public thing") which might just "halt the cycle of [political] change and decline."[11]

The problem with republics past and present is their conflation of durability with conquest and empire (as though the best defense was a strong offence). The Roman Empire was present in nascent form throughout the centuries of the Republic, struggling to come into being, just as the imperial ambitions of France and America have been part and parcel of their republics, too. The "mixture" of kings, aristocrats, and commoners in a republic is never a balanced or equal mix: the first two classes almost always comprise a wealthy and powerful 1% exploiting an excluded (slaves and plebes) and or diverted (bread and circuses) 99%.

Set these two quotations beside each other, as the paradoxical portal through which we must pass in this contemplation – a portal opening onto a public square where an old man, the voice of the commons, comes to present his complaint ("The government has annihilated any hope for my survival and I could not get any justice. I cannot find any other form of struggle except a dignified end before I have to start scrounging for food from the trash"[12]) – and make his horrible protest:

> [Virgil:] Romans, keep in mind that your art form is government.[13]

> [Walter Benjamin:] There is no document of culture that is not at the same time a document of barbarism.[14]

★

April 23

The decline and fall of Rome was the natural
and inevitable effect of immoderate greatness.
Prosperity ripened the principle of decay; the
causes of destruction multiplied with the
extent of conquest; and as soon as time or
accident had removed the artificial supports,
the stupendous fabric yielded to the pressure
of its own weight.

– EDWARD GIBBON
The Decline and Fall of the Roman Empire

Writing Rome's history in the eighteenth century, while sitting in
the midst of its ruins, Edward Gibbon might merely be picking up
on "the ancient tendency to exalt the past over the present and to
think of change as degenerative."[15] Or perhaps he is giving expression to a sort of cultural version of the second law of thermodynamics – the idea of entropy – that all ordered systems devolve
toward disorder, that everything begins and ends in chaos.

Polybius – a Greek writing in Rome – gives this idea its classical
political formulation:

> Monarchy first changes into its vicious allied form,
> tyranny; and next, the abolishment of both gives
> birth to aristocracy. Aristocracy by its very nature
> degenerates into oligarchy; and when the commons
> inflamed by anger takes vengeance on this govern-
> ment for its unjust rule, democracy comes into
> being; and in due course the licence and lawlessness

of this form of government produces mob-rule to complete the series ... Such is the cycle of political revolution, the course appointed by nature in which constitutions change, disappear, and finally return to the point from which they started.[16]

Polybius seemingly describes an endless cycle (and a "natural" one at that – discussions of change almost always conflate the "natural" and the "social" in some way) – but really, it is a downward spiral, "the change for the worse that is sure to follow."[17] Walk among the ruins of Rome – stumble upon what is left of the Hadrianeum (amid the ruins of which, in 1695, was a customs house) or the Portico di Ottavia, or better, what little remains of the Forum itself, or the forum of Julius Caesar, largely buried under the traffic of the Via dei Fori Imperiali, and tell me the law of entropy does not apply to civilizations.

Rome, most likely, exhausted the carrying capacity of its environment, experiencing overshoot. All civilizations fall, all human development comes up against the limits of what the natural environment can be made to provide and sustain. The best state, it was thought, is that which resists inevitable decline the longest (or, rarely, discovers its limits and works to sustain itself within them). But like biological life forms, such durability is best achieved through serial reproduction (of governments and States), rather than through the durability of the individual unit (which inevitably dies). This is the amazing invention of life: that it is able to "last" while "dying," enduring via the reproducibility of its fragile and short-lived individual units. Democracy may be the social expression of this: governments "die" as new governments are "born." The reproduction of democracies is supposed to be the free and open election – though these are rare enough, and certainly we are yet to find the ideal mechanism for the "reproduction" of the self-rule of the commons. Such discoveries await us – if we can sustain our presence on this planet long enough.

★

April 24

Everywhere in Rome the powerful put their stamp on things, sometimes counting coup where an earlier potentate had already beat them to it. There's nothing a pope wouldn't put a plaque on, announcing his munificence or eternal grandeur, and emperors' statues vie with those of the gods (apparently Augustus had twenty thousand marble images of himself decorating the city). The wealth of even the smallest church is astounding (most, in Rome, can boast of a Caravaggio or two). Outside, immigrants from all over the world illegally hawk the most banal and unappealing junk, desperate to make enough money to buy food for another day, quite possibly entrapped in some contemporary version of indentured servitude.

We walk through the Campo de Fiori at night, and it is an open square. Returning the next morning, it is filled with stalls selling fruit, vegetables, and, yes, flowers. In the middle of the square stands the imposing statue of Giordano Bruno, burned here in 1600 for teaching that "the universe, far from being the tight and limited system of concentric spheres conceived by medieval cosmogony, all tied into orbit around their Unmoved Mover, was in fact infinitely large"[18] – and, perhaps just as importantly, was without a center.

Any system (whether political or cosmological) – in order to counteract entropy, to work against the pull of decay and disorder – needs to be open, needs to open onto an outside and have access to a source of free energy there.[19] It cannot persist otherwise – cannot grow or be sustained. This is true of an organic being as it is of the Roman Empire or contemporary capitalism. What is the politics of the open system? It should be horizontal, participatory, decentralized, modular. All power to its soviets, which pulse in and out of existence like neurons firing in the collective brain.

Should be. But rarely is. Capitalism has learned a trick: create new "outsides" through creative destruction (the intentional degradation, marginalization, or suppression of certain regions), and then you don't have to worry – just wear the mask of democracy and inclusion, while you continue centralizing and excluding, colonizing and decolonizing. But the planet is only so large, and can bear the burden of only so much intentional (and unintentional) destruction.

The key is in how one relates to one's much-needed outside, onto which one's system necessarily opens and upon which it depends. Does the open system exploit its outside – its "externalities" – leaving exhaustion and destruction in its wake, as capitalism and Empire do? Or does it have a symbiotic relationship with it, a relationship of gift exchange and sustainability, of stewardship or trusteeship?

The "free market," it's worth noting, never has been "free" – it is maintained artificially as an outside into which unequal actors stride like gladiators, or around which the idle aristocracy recline to place bets, simultaneously incurring and erasing debts.

The Forum, theoretically, was an open space into which virtually anyone could come and speak, and find an audience. "Mic check!" Today, poppies grow in the grass amidst the fragments of stone. Contrast the Forum's "openness" with the Pantheon's imperial "enclosure," its "symmetry … contrived because it had to be: the imperial message was order itself."[20] Geometric patterns of circles and squares abound in the quintessential imperial building. The number seven governs almost everything: seven main alcoves in the first level, 14 niches in the intermediate band (one for each day we will be in Rome, my wife, Cathy, reminds). The coffers pocketing the dome are five rows of 28, for a total of 140. The dome is 140 feet across, its oculus a perfect 140 feet from the floor (and 28 feet across its opening).

In what was the Saepta Julia, I look across at the Pantheon and down at the square where voices never cease, music plays, and swallows spin through the air. Voting was replaced by games –

participation replaced by spectacle – the market of ideas erased by the market of wares. The bedazzled were invited to stare into the dome, "lost in an incommensurable void."[21] How far are we now from ancient Rome? How much have we actually changed?

★

April 25

The dialectics of the Pantheon: everywhere the symbolism of circle and square – even to the point where the building itself is a great sphere sunk in a giant block, half circle, half square. Oculus (circle) surrounded by coffers (squares) – and the chessboard of alternating circles and squares in the floor – even the combination of portico (square) and dome (circle) was unique when it was built, "at a turning point in history, when rites and rules drawn from a very long past were not yet abandoned, but when the surge of a new and utterly different age was already being felt."[22]

And then there is the dialectic of love and strife – Venus and Mars. Dio Cassius, in one of the earliest literary accounts of the Pantheon, names only these two among "statues of many gods" present on and in the building.[23] Rome was founded upon a fratricide – Romulus killing his brother Remus, strife where there should have been love – but more than this, the Trojan line of mythical founders traces its heritage to Venus, mother of Aeneas, while Romulus and Remus are said to have been sired by Mars. So love and strife entwine everywhere in Rome's self-mythologizing – as they do, perhaps, in the very notion of "civilization" and the "State," the creation and maintenance of which (not to mention the colonial expansion thereof) is built upon a dialectic of inclusion and exclusion, of (supposedly) *caring-for* and (decidedly) *persecuting*.

The Greek philosopher Empedocles saw Love and Strife as the motor of change: "The creator and maker of the generation of all generated things is deadly Strife, while the change and departure of generated things from the world and the establishment of the One is the work of Love" – a process apparently governed by "the change of one to many by Strife and from many to one by Love."[24]

This concept is given its political expression by Jean-Pierre Vernant: "The spirit of conflict and the spirit of union – Eris-Philia: these two divine entities, opposed and complementary, marked the two poles of society in the aristocratic world that followed the ancient kingships."[25] Vernant here refers to the advent of the democratic era that, in ancient Greece as in ancient Rome, followed the end of the rule of kings – an era of struggle and negotiation between aristocratic elites and the commons.

The commons is the force of unity – a unity, paradoxically, in multiplicity, the bringing of all into one great whole – while the elites, whether monarchial, aristocratic, imperial, or corporate, are the forces of division, splitting off the social fraction and drawing a vastly disproportionate share of power and wealth to the few, dividing, distracting, and dispersing the many so they cannot cohere and rise against them.

None of which – even the cosmological version where gravity (attraction: Love) combats universal expansion and entropy (dissipation: Strife) – is to say that the dialectical motor of class conflict is entirely inevitable, irresolvable, and eternally cyclical. The question – *the* political question perhaps – is how best to manage the dialectic of conflict and union, minority and majority, strife and love. By what mechanism or process? Under the aegis of what definition of the social totality and the common wealth? Key, here, is the realization that we have not yet ever found the ultimate (good for all times and places) solution to this problem. Nor will we. "Is a democracy," Thoreau asks in *Resistance to Civil Government*, "such as we have known it, the last possible improvement in government?"[26] The key is to keep trying, to keep refashioning the social network, like neurons which are never fixed, but fire their evanescent connections with each new thought and sensation, plastically adapting themselves to new habits of thought.

★

April 26

Rome is a most public city. Everything appears to happen in the streets – love, business, fighting, singing, eating, and drinking. Water is its ultimate expression of publicness – baths in ancient Rome, fountains now in modern Rome. We share our waters – our dependence upon them, our shared condition of being water-beings. Water's boundaries are not fixed, not easily divisible into *mine* and *thine*. "*Volemose bene*" – let's take care of each other – a Roman politician once said.

> What was distinctive about the Republic was that the crowd, which met in the Forum to hear speeches and then to vote, was itself, once formed into voting units, the *sovereign* body, and the only one that could legislate … Republican Rome was a direct democracy … in which the sovereign power really was held by "the Roman People."[27]

Ideally – but in actual fact? I think Rome, perhaps inadvertently, let this idea loose into the world – though the idea is yet to truly find full, material, social implementation. However that may be, we are returning to such utopian notions, out of necessity. As Rousseau noted, "Nothing is more dangerous in public affairs than the influence of private interests."[28] This is now more the case than ever. The modern era – the era of revolutionary change, driven by the re-entry of "the people" into the realm of public affairs – arrived with reference to the Roman Republic. Now, as the occupations carry on their work in countless cities around the world, the ancient Roman "requirement of publicity … that a range of public acts should be performed 'under the gaze of the *populus Romanus*'" is also of renewed importance.[29] Social change only happens when its crucial moves are made in public – in the open air of the town square. When we really all start to notice *what's actually going on*, and what our share in the process is. When we accept the idea that there is such a thing as "the public," and recognize our role and responsibility *in constituting it.*

Our public spaces began as markets, and quickly became evolving centers of political exchange. How to make the market, once more, an agora? How can we replace the abstraction of "exchange value" with the material reality and "use value" of participatory democracy – as the center and raison d'être of our societies?

Yet our evocations of past political models and ideals – the Roman Republic and its Forum, the Athenian Agora – are tinged with the ironies of their startling … imperfections. Slavery. The exclusion of women. Empire building. Why is it that all the great "democracies" of history, the ancient originators and the revolutionary republics, were also colonizers and exploiters, champions of privilege and expanding markets? We've never quite got it right – always raising a racket at the door that never but partly opens, admitting only a few. Still we call for the door to be thrown from its hinges, for its hinges to be torn from the jam. Change begins when we stream into the streets, when we take the square – when we make our shared concerns a question of *public* "safety" and the *common* "wealth." When there isn't really any way to avoid what's inescapably occurring *in public.*

Democracy must ultimately be separated from State and corporation. It must become what the commons *does*, on a daily basis.

★

April 27

Nine days in Rome. Ruins and art. The graves of poets. The cool and dark interior of the Curia where the Roman Senate met, at the side of the Forum – was the ceiling so high to remind the wealthy and privileged who assembled there of their relative insignificance in a vast universe? The frozen moment of Bernini's *Daphne and Apollo* – the girl halfway between human and tree – why haven't I written about this? Today I stood in front of Garofalo's *Circe Transforms Picus into a Woodpecker* in the Palazzo Barberini. The witch touches the unfortunate man with her wand, and he is depicted mid-transformation – top half bird, bottom half man. But her wand is also a paintbrush, and she is *painting* Picus into a bird, allowing us to reflect on the transformative power of art. Culture *is* change – is a mode of managing and provoking change – our key adaptation as human beings, evolved to facilitate faster and more varied responses to a changing world.

I will, in the coming days, produce something of a taxonomy of – or more accurately, a fairly idiosyncratic, non-linear series of "theses" on – the history of change: its mechanics, its historical expression and conception, its various framings and implications. I hope to offer something useful for those wanting to think through the problem of change, the possibilities of navigating change. Of *producing* change, if that is possible in a world already governed by change and regimes of change management.

Indeed, it seems that change is the hallmark
for the origin, maintenance, and fate of all
things, animate or inanimate.

– ERIC CHAISSON
Cosmic Evolution

THESIS 1

**Change occurs, dialectically, at both the "natural" and "social"
(cultural) levels, in a kind of dynamic feedback loop.** "Natural"
(or environmental) conditions prompt social (or cultural)
adaptations, which in turn fire further changes in the natural
environment.

> [David Harvey:] We cannot transform what's going
> on around us without transforming ourselves. Con-
> versely, we can't transform ourselves without trans-
> forming everything going on around us ... This
> dialectic, of perpetually transforming oneself by
> transforming the world and vice versa, is funda-
> mental to understanding the evolution of human
> societies as well as the evolution of nature itself.[30]

Today, that loop is tightening as the changes we wreak on the
natural world are rapidly undermining and destabilizing the realm
of the social and the cultural, which must adapt all the more
quickly. It's difficult now not to think in terms of an apocalypse.
What has characterized us as a species is our ability tò change when
faced with an unpredictably and often precipitously changing
world. Have we lost this ability? Our political and economic system
seems more sclerotic and unmoving than ever before – even
though it has evolved on principles of "innovation" and rapid
adjustment to an ever-changing global "market."

The social and natural are not really separate or separable. In the mid-nineteenth century, Darwin used economic language (describing genetic adaptations as "profitable") and Marx used biological language (the "social metabolism" of labor) to describe processes of change in the natural and social worlds, respectively. The human being stands in a vortex of forces, a constant feedback loop of genetic and cultural evolution. In *Not by Genes Alone*, Richerson and Boyd assert that "*culture is part of biology*."[31] The social and the cultural evolved through adaptation – just like all adaptation that occurs within biological processes. Culture is an extension of our biology – but a unique and, well, *strange* extension.

Human evolution is a *social* evolution; all of our history is, essentially, a history of social movement and social change. What we specifically call "social movements" are moments of self-consciousness about this general pattern and fact – moments when we become aware that we are *engines* of *change*, and can in fact engage our agency (collectively) and to some extent direct our own course, our own "movement."

THESIS 2

Another version of this same dialectic: generally, **change is governed by the interaction of external and internal transformations** – changes which apparently come from *outside* ourselves and over which we feel we have relatively little control, and changes we ourselves apparently initiate *internally*, via our agency and will. Sometimes, historically, one or the other pole is emphasized.

The Roman discourse of "fortune" and divine interference is a version of "external" change. Polybius contended that "Fortune has steered almost all the affairs of the world in one direction and forced them to converge on one and the same goal" (that goal being the foundation and supremacy of Rome). Similarly, Appian glossed political turmoil by observing that, "It would seem that the divine will was interfering with public affairs to bring about change."[32]

In times of revolution and rapid mass social change, it seems to be the pole of agency that becomes ascendant. Actually, the gap narrows, the dialectic tightens, becomes very dynamic, oscillatory, a quickly relaying feedback loop. We feel at once intense *external pressures* (debt, climate change, economic collapse), and the urgent need and facility to *act* (to institute emergency measures, to take to the streets in mass demonstration). At the same time, *internal* changes (of opinion, a rising sense that one *can act* because one *must act*) coalesce, become collective, and thus seemingly "external" again, a social "movement" we become "swept up in" (as external forces in turn draw us together in our common plight).

Politics are, or ought to be, the realm of "changes we can make" – the coming together of our various agencies, in public. However, too often politics seem to be "changes that befall us," over which we have no control and in which we have no say ("I didn't vote for *this* ..."). When the political realm becomes so configured, when it comes to be dominated by policies legislated *against* us and actions taken to constrain us, it is in crisis.

Today, the student of the history of change ponders the imbrications of inside/outside, "man-made" and environmentally determined. Today, to study change is to attempt to understand, and to forestall, the collapse of the entire human project. The changes we must understand now are world changes, system changes.

Today, the student of the history of change knows that we must learn and act quickly, that these are revolutionary times we are living through, prepared for through long struggle – and through long periods of forgetting, long tracts of ignorance and willful delusion, of distraction and being "bought off," of debt servitude and a wage-labor system that is often indistinguishable from slavery, numbing minds and bodies and molding the will into something pliable, or chaining it to a wall of psychological doubt and fear, terror and alienation.

L. Nathan Oaklander offers a third version of this dialectic. "The problem of change," he says "arises out of a conflict of intuitions. On the one hand change requires *sameness*. A thing that changes must be one and the same both before and after the change ... On the other hand, change requires *difference*."[33]

Change is thus a dialectic of sameness and difference, a phenomenon that can show both these qualities at once. That which changes endures, but betrays some transformation. Without both these qualities, we cannot notice that a change has occurred.

The driver of change today – in *all* social, cultural, and material ways – is capitalism and its seemingly objective ("the market"), self-perpetuating, and solipsistic mechanisms. The capitalist system's ability to adapt, "innovatively," to the rapid changes in market conditions that it, itself, releases reveals an almost indistinguishable interaction of difference (creative destruction: old markets collapse and new markets open) and sameness (the market, ultimately, always "wins" – whether bear or bull, money is made somewhere in the system when it is lost elsewhere in the system; capitalism is indifferent to *who*, specifically, profits, so long as there is growth).

Thus change now is driven by this ruthless abstraction – the market, "futures," "growth" – and the structure of interest-bearing debts driving these – all of which obscure the fact of very real, material environmental destruction and human suffering. But capitalism does not exist in an infinite space – it is not without limits, despite its tendency toward the limitless – thus its assumed, self-perpetuating "sameness" (constant growth) has a date with an ultimate "difference" (a combined, global economic and ecological crisis), which will be the real game changer. Resources run out and the environment can only bear so much exploitation and pollution. The capitalist system is in the process of separating difference from sameness – by indifferently sawing off the branch it is sitting on.

The dialectic of sameness and difference underwriting change also relates to another transformative imaginary: Utopia. "The fundamental dynamic of any Utopian politics," Fredric Jameson writes in *Archaeologies of the Future*, lies "in the dialectic of Identity and Difference, to the degree to which such politics aims at imagining, and sometimes even at realizing, a system radically different from this one."[34] Thus our attempts to generate and facilitate change, which so often depend upon the availability of, or ability to produce, utopian visions of alternative systems and worlds, also by necessity both invoke a familiar sameness (today's world wracked by crisis) and a contrasting difference (another possible world that does not generate such crises).

Capitalism is built on a logic of perpetual change. And it does betray "utopian" characteristics (its impossible vision of limitless growth). But the real difference between capitalism and utopia lies in the fact that capitalism's change always masks an unremitting sameness (more growth, more inequality), while utopia's change is premised on the idea of a fundamental alteration of the status quo.

★

April 28

Efforts to effect social change – like all other aspects of the social – are cumulative. We are not starting from scratch, but building upon the accumulated tactics and social knowledge of our predecessors: anti-globalization protesters; Zapatistas; Greenpeace activists; Red Brigades and Autonomists; anti-Vietnam and antinuke protestors; civil rights activists; feminists and proto-feminists; labor unionists; suffragettes; abolitionists; socialist, communist, and anarchist parties, unions and movements, etc. All offer various modalities of resistance and revolution that can help us adapt to our changing world circumstances and the structures of State and corporate power in the here and now.

Sometimes I am asked – usually by someone not exactly supportive of the Occupy movement – how I can justify civil disobedience. I dutifully recall for them the fact that so many of the benefits we take for granted in Western democracies, from the forty-hour work week and eight-hour day, to medical coverage, employment insurance, workplace health and safety measures, anti-discrimination laws, among many other now-fraying strands in the once-robust social safety net, are the legacy of past social movements that engaged in acts of civil disobedience. This inheritance of social benefits is increasingly threatened by "austerity" measures intended to protect corporate profits and punish the commons for market excess. The point here is that everything in human society – both good and bad, as well as the "establishment" and the "counterculture" – has accumulated over time, building upon past endeavors to protect or redress privilege.

Cultural adaptations (social changes), Richerson and Boyd argue, are "assembled by the gradual accumulation of small variations like organic adaptations" – which is how "most cultural change occurs." Within the process of transformation, "no single innovator contributes more than a small portion of the total, as any single gene substitution contributes only marginally to a complex organic adaptation."[35]

Change, Clive Ponting notes in *A New Green History of the World*, thus operates via a "ratchet effect."[36] Each small shift builds upon the last, so that over time a small adjustment can seem to have a disproportionate effect and catalytic power. This is sometimes referred to as a "tipping point."

The accumulation of a surplus – of extra food and necessities, which can then be distributed in some way to people who have not done the work of acquiring the food or necessities – is the basis for what we have called "civilization." Ponting asserts that "food surplus … was the foundation of all later social and political change … In the broadest framework human history over the last 8,000 years has been about the acquisition and distribution of this surplus food and the uses to which it has been put."[37]

A surplus allows for the maintenance of scribes, artists, priests, soldiers. A food surplus buys time to think, invent, and imagine – or to conquer, exterminate, and colonize. Human culture, at a very basic level, is the result of accumulated surpluses over a long stretch of time ("recorded history"). This is why accumulation and surplus play such crucial roles in Marx's analysis of capitalism. They are what it – and dreams – are made of.

The accumulation of capital is undertaken at the expense of the commons, for the benefit of elites. The social surplus is contained and controlled, access to it regulated and exploited. The accumulation of cultural adaptations (art and ideas) is also under-written by privilege (the control and distribution of surpluses), and often subject to elite, private accumulation (the museums of Rome, many of which are former palaces, abound with artwork commissioned by and dedicated to wealthy patrons) – but it slips through the fingers of private accumulation like water. Culture is harder to contain than capital because it is more or less inalienable, a part of the human inheritance, like our genome – our language, ideas, and stories are not so easily taken from us once they have taken hold. But the attempt to privatize and control them is made nonetheless, and is thus an important ground of struggle – if we are to retain our transformative agency.

To claim that "you cannot evict an idea whose time has come" is to make a statement about the inalienable nature of ideas. They cannot be *evicted* because they cannot be *owned*: they are our common accumulated patrimony. The uncontrollable nature of ideas is the greatest strength and resource of the commons. Even when it becomes difficult to hold on to physical space, we might yet hold on to the space of ideas and debate. Ultimately, we have our own accumulated and inalienable intellectual surplus, with which we oppose capitalism's accumulated material surplus.

THESIS 5

> As the size and variety of information
> networks grow, we should expect to find
> not just an accumulation of new knowledge
> but an *acceleration* in the accumulation of
> new knowledge.
>
> – DAVID CHRISTIAN
> *Maps of Time*

We often have the perception that things are changing faster all the time. That the lag between social and generational shifts is shrinking. This is in fact accurate. **Acceleration and accumulation go hand in hand in the dynamics of change**.

"Cultural evolution," Chaisson writes, "acts much faster than biological evolution"[38] – which may be why it evolved in the first place (the human advantage: to use culture as a means of adapting more quickly to changing environmental circumstances). The danger with this is that the development of agriculture, then fossil fuels, allowed us to slam down the social accelerator, even though we have not been able to adapt quickly enough to the changing environmental circumstances *that we, paradoxically, created!*

Cultural evolution also leads to a situation where the speed of "technologically driven changes" outstrips the ability of the biosphere to keep up and compensate with its own evolutionary changes: our "cultural advantage" becomes a great biological disadvantage, when looked at from the perspective of the entire biosphere (which we are now able to effect directly – that is – *destroy*).[39]

> [E.J. Hughes (*Environmental History of the World*):] If there is any judgment historians can make about technological change, it is that its pace is accelerating at a rate never previously matched, and that its environmental impacts are similarly escalating. That pace has outstripped a traditional human method of coping with environmental change through gradually altering taboos and customs.[40]

> [Ponting:] The problem for modern societies is the scale and interlinked nature of the magnitude of environmental challenges they face, the speed with which economic, technological and social change is taking place and the lack of effective mechanisms to deal with these issues.[41]

Thus the reason for, and perhaps the necessity of, things such as the Slow Food movement. We need to slow everything down. The accelerator in culture is not an absolute necessity. Rather, it is a side effect of cultural evolution that we can and must learn to adjust and curtail (if we can catch up to it!), rather than continue to abuse, like some teenager on joyride in his father's new Porsche. Here we also find a key aspect of the Occupy movement: sit down in your town square now and STOP. Figure out how and why we are doing things the way we are, and how and why we might do them differently. Resist the forward momentum of business as usual. Another world is only possible if we take the time – and expend the surplus – on planning for it, thinking and imagining it, and carefully building it.

Up escalators and down escalators: **the history of change as an intellectual subject has been written between the push and pull of models suggesting a steady decline and models optimistically predicting steady and irrefutable "progress."** Even cyclical models (such as those favored by the ancient Greeks) still chart one's position as either on the up- or downslope. States of equilibrium are always temporary, fleeting, fragile. What appears to be at "rest" is actually composed, at some level, of constant transformation, movement, and the active tension of dialectical forces; in Heraclitus's oft-quoted words, "You can never step in the same river twice." The reasons for this seem to relate to the nature of the universe itself and the atomic materials we, and everything else, are made of. (Whenever I despair over particularly chaotic moments in my life, I like to remind myself: you're living in the midst, or aftermath, of a vast universal explosion – how much "stability" can you expect?)

> [Christian:] Creating and sustaining patterns means working against this apparently universal tendency towards disorder … Whatever the source of order, its creation … requires creating structures that can channel and control large flows of energy without falling apart. This is an extremely difficult trick. And that difficulty explains why ordered entities are fragile and rare … Paradoxically, the tendency toward increasing entropy – the drive toward disorder – may itself be the engine that creates order. It creates order *on the way* to creating disorder.[42]

Christian is referencing the second law of thermodynamics, which Chaisson contends "has perhaps the most to say about the concept of change."[43] The universe is a massive release of energy, and the tendency of that energy release is toward dissipation. Whether we're talking about a star, a jellyfish, or a social movement, we're talking about a structure devised to channel and "order" the flow of energy, and (temporarily) harness it before it dissipates – to make "order" out of – and on the way to – "chaos."[44]

Shifting scales slightly: a social revolution could be said to create *disorder* on the way to creating a *new social order* – all the while nested in the larger patters of social order formation within the universal tendency toward entropic disorder. Complexity is by definition unstable.

> [Christian:] That the most complex structures break down so fast is a measure of the difficulty of managing particularly dense energy flows: this is the price living organisms pay for their aggressive challenge to the second law of thermodynamics … Unlike stars or crystals, which are general, all-purpose antientropy machines, living organisms can adapt constantly to new terrain and new challenges in their more flexible guerrilla war on entropy … What they find is new sources of energy and new ways of organizing themselves so as to survive the hurricane of energy flowing through them.[45]

So every structure is a bulwark against the forces that are destined to disintegrate it. The more complex the structure, the more precise and specialized and adaptable its order-producing mechanisms can be – but consequently the more fragile and short-lived it is (generally, from a cosmological perspective). Our societies are probably the most complex structures ever to exist in the universe, and their means of organizing energy flows ("economics" and "politics") the most varied and "plastic" forms of complex adaptation, transforming constantly in order to stay ahead of the game. It is the nature of life to challenge and resist entropy – this "resistance" is exactly what evolution describes. The idea that we could reach a point of social fixity is contrary to the basic principles of the universe. Change is always what social activity and interaction is "about." Politics is the facilitation of transformation.

Fighting a losing battle might not sound very inviting – but all life ends in death. In the meantime, what we build to channel the constant flow of energy through everything that exists is the springboard to a future that can continue the anti-entropic effort. Biological life evolved a different anti-entropic method than the non-organic: reproduction, by which an ordered structure achieves durability not through the simplicity of its structure (like a star, which is almost pure helium and hydrogen, and lasts for billions of years of intense energy release), but, via its short-lived but reproductive complexity.

What can we learn about change here? All structures – from the cosmic to the organic to the social – are methods of managing change and producing temporary, local durability in a universe governed by entropy. We might ask, are our social structures actually fulfilling their anti-entropic function? Our current society manages the greatest energy flows of any human-generated structure in history, but there are signs everywhere of the entropic breakdown of this system, of its tendency not to thwart, but to *accelerate* entropy, and its failure to reproduce itself into a viable future. We are, ultimately, as much change managers as changemakers; how can we be better stewards of the changing world we inhabit, produce, order, and reorder?

★

April 29

The future is here already – It's just not
evenly distributed yet.

— WILLIAM GIBSON

Change always involves a differential – an uneven development –
an "unorganized" place from which "free energy" can be acquired,
and into which waste energy can be spilled. When human societies
institutionalize this process broadly, base their means of production upon its maximization and make of it both a means and
an end (capitalism), problems begin to accumulate, as the search
for free energy, and the disposal of waste energy, becomes
increasingly compulsive, frenetic, and difficult to sustain.

   We are still in the grip of entropy here, and the pressure upon
systems to create and maintain order within the general tendency
toward disorder. "Industrial development," Chaisson argues,
"decreases entropy locally … [but] inevitably increases entropy in
the larger environment" – by both stripping energy from and
disposing waste in a space marked as "outside" the particular
system.[46] Order only exists in the midst of disorder – a local
pattern amidst the more general pattern – but it always erodes
toward the equilibrium point of disorder. "Localized, open systems
can be sites of emergent order within a global (i.e., universal)
environment that is largely and increasingly disordered."[47]

   The global politics of this, as outlined by Ponting: "The way in
which one part of the world – western Europe, North America

and the white settlement colonies – became 'developed' and the way in which another part became 'underdeveloped' are not separate phenomena."[48]

The uneven development of socio-economic systems leads inevitably to conflict and crisis.

> [Wolfgang Streeck:] Mainstream economics has tended to conceive society as governed by a general tendency toward equilibrium, where crises and change are no more than temporary deviations from the steady state of a normally well-integrated system [when in reality there is] a basic underlying tension in the political-economic configuration of advanced-capitalist societies; a tension which makes disequilibrium and instability the rule rather than the exception … a condition ruled by an endemic conflict between capitalist markets and democratic politics.[49]

Thus the uneven development and the social and economic inequality that capitalism systemically depends upon is mirrored by the uneven development of capitalism and democracy, the full development of the former requiring an underdevelopment (and ultimate ineffectiveness) of the latter. This is quite simply because the "freedom" of markets does not in most cases uphold or protect the "freedom" of either individuals or communities (the commons), laissez-faire rhetoric to the contrary. Capitalism has one raison d'être and one only – to continue growing – and this is not the same as democracy's distributive function, which seeks out horizontal networks of reciprocal codependence and a balancing of consenting "interests."

To explain what comes to bear in an instance we want to define as **"change" requires that we examine an array of interpenetrating factors, because we are *overdetermined* beings**. It is the complex interaction of history, genetics, environment, culture – gender, race, religion, class, sexuality, social status – technology, education, experience, chance – nation, geography, language – that surrounds the fickle flicker of individuality and composes what we call "agency," opening the door to the possibilities that we may act as *conscious changemakers*.

The Italian anarchist Bartolomeo Vanzetti offers one of the best descriptions of this *overdetermination* amidst which a thoroughly "conditioned" agency and will continues, nevertheless and even paradoxically, to persist. Writing from jail, awaiting execution for a crime he did not commit, he explains his basic philosophy to his correspondent. "I believe to have been [born] with the faculties of acquiring ideas, forming opinions, learning words, and express myself – but not with opinions, ideas and words already in me."[50]

The impressions made by both genetic and lived, environmental "conditions" are extensive, and Vanzetti offers a brief overview, in his broken and unique English.

> I am but too well aware, alas! to have begun as a miser to have inherited all the misery of the earth and of the race, called atavism – to have been taken to church when I was wholly unconscious and irresponsible, to have been spiritually raped by the priests, when I was wholly unable to defend myself, to have been intellectually warped and poisoned by the State school, when I was unable to discriminate – to have grown within a humanity so stupid, ignorant, vile, coward, arrogant, self-conceited, brutal, greedy, ferocious and filthy and falsely proud and humble, that the best of my essence was choked in myself, or, what is still worse, distorted and aberated.[51]

Vanzetti comes close to Rousseau's idea of a natural, savage nobility warped and distorted by socialization – except Vanzetti's account is somewhat more nuanced and complex. He goes on to claim a difficult and long-struggled-for self "rinnovation," a growing awareness of the forces that have shaped who he is, via a counter-inheritance acquired from "many humble persons and children who gave me fragments of truth." He continues: "All what I have said may induce you to believe that I am a so-called 'Determinist.' I am not so, though I believe in the existence of a 'together of things' which we pass through and which influence in a 'concomittant' factor of our individuality."[52]

This "together of things" includes those "genetic" faculties and proclivities, as well as the environmental conditioning referred to above – nature, nurture, and, Vanzetti adds, like a good Darwinian, "chance" – unpredictable "changes and conditions that alter" the other factors. Thus Vanzetti's "together of things" leads him to "believe to a certain extent in both [free will and determinism], as limited and changeable phenomenum, interdependent."[53]

Contemporary philosophy would tend to agree. "Free will," according to Daniel Dennett, has "evolved" in the complex matrix of nature, nurture, and chance. "It appears to be a stable and ahistorical construct, as eternal and unchanging as arithmetic, but it is not."[54] Rather, free will is "an evolved creation of human activity and beliefs," which makes it "just as real" – and just as plastic – "as such other human creations as music and money."[55]

Life-forms have endured over many millennia by adapting modes of "harm avoidance," the more complex the life-form the more complex the modes of harm avoidance. Human beings, especially, have evolved a multifaceted system of decision making to anticipate and negotiate potential harms. "There are two requirements for a meaningful choice," Dennett notes: "information and a path for the information to guide."[56] What the individual human being does with this information is open to something we may want to call agency, as the nature/nurture/chance matrix rarely offers only one path around a potential harm. Complexity – not determination but *overdetermination* – leads to diversity and multiplicity, which at once conditions and benefits a life-form able to "choose" among available options.[57]

Change is always about the future – we cannot change the past, but changes we instigate today may indeed lead to an altered formation of the "now" tomorrow. Of course, in a very literal sense you can't "change the future" – the future will be the way it "is" once we arrive "there." But we can alter modes of social relations and social structures "now" that can shape a future which functions in markedly different ways than "today" and the trajectory we imagine "today" to take toward the future.

> [While] Mother Nature is herself lacking in foresight, she has managed to create beings – us human beings, preeminently – who do have foresight, and are even beginning to put this foresight to use in guiding and abetting the very process of natural selection on this planet … Culture provides the vantage point from which we can see how to change the trajectories into the future that have been laid down by the blind explorations of our genes.[58]

In the end, "free will" may itself in part be a matter of "choice" (though a multifaceted, conditioned "choice"): if you *believe* you are free to act as you so choose, you will most likely do so, but if you believe you are *not* free to act as you desire, you will most likely not. There is much in our world that has lulled us into a false sense of being "determined." We need, desperately, to rediscover both the actual limits and potentialities of our wills.[59]

★

April 30

Plasticity is perhaps the primary characteristic of the human species – the very slipperiness of our species being. Richerson and Boyd note that "humans are much more variable than any other species of animal … Any theory that hopes to explain the behavior of contemporary humans *must* tell us what it is that causes humans to be so much more variable than any other species and why this particular capacity for variation was favored by natural selection."[60]

Answer: culture. The evolved ability to learn by example, to pass on information, in increasing complexity and amounts, outside of genetic inheritance, and the social organization that this innovation requires and instigates. "Culture is a system of inheriting acquired variation."[61] But this is only part of the answer. What might have prompted the innovation of culture?

Answer: climate change. "Social learning is an adaptation to increased climate variation during the last half of the Pleistocene" – a period of "stunning … climate deterioration" and "cyclical patterns of glacial advance and retreat" which can be "correlated with increases in brain size in many mammalian lineages."[62]

Intelligence is an adaptation "to manage a complex social life," favoring "the evolution of a sophisticated ability to take the perspective of others," thus making "imitation possible, launching the evolution of the most elementary form of complex cultural traditions."[63] Richerson and Boyd go on to argue that social learning and genetics function in a feedback loop, each propelling the other along at an accelerated rate, and transforming human begins into truly remarkable agents of transformation: "the symbiosis between genes and culture in the human species has led to … the evolution of complex cooperative human societies that radically transformed almost all the world's habitats over the last ten thousand years."[64]

Crucial in terms of what evolved in a new way in our species was the transformative capacity of the human brain. Norman Doidge, in *The Brain That Changes Itself*, writes about the brain's exceptional neuroplasticity: "The brain is a far more open system than we ever imagined, and nature has gone very far to help us perceive and take in the world around us. It has given us a brain that survives in a changing world by changing itself."[65]

The "brain is constantly adapting itself," Doidge continues, and "we can change our brain anatomy simply by using our imaginations" – because, "from a neuroscientific point of view, imagining an act and doing it are not as different than they sound."[66]

The neurological fact of plasticity, the evolutionary fact of human variability and the cumulative and acceleratory aspects of social learning all determine the capriciousness and idiosyncratic agency of the human. Let no one ever claim we cannot change – we are in fact change personified, Promethean and protean to the core. We are, it seems, unique among species in our ability to imagine a change, and then effect some version of that change through our actions. If we sometimes seem to have lost the ability to engage the world directly, feeling instead powerless in the face of the vast mechanical forces of economics, politics, and history, such passivity is *learned* behavior. We can and need to train ourselves back out of it.

The question is, in the middle of another wave of climate change (this time triggered by our own activities), can we use our plasticity to alter our course quickly enough, and transform our selves and societies? Such a transformation is of a new meta-order: it requires us to become the conscious stewards of our own transformative powers.

THESIS 10

The advent of democracy was an innovation amid rapid and destabilizing social change – an attempt to find a way to harness opposing forces into a system that could be driven forward by their sustained tension. **Democracy is a social change regulator** (as opposed to political systems that are largely intended to be change resistors and stasis promoters). Democracy embraces disorder as a means of creating order – takes decentralization and distribution as a means of creating social cohesion.

This is, more or less, Jean-Pierre Vernant's argument in his classic *The Origins of Greek Thought*. The fall of Mycenaean civilization and its system of monarchial hierarchy left a void in which the forces of the commons and the warrior aristocracy struggled for control. The solution was the polis and the radical, rational thought associated with it. Vernant explains how

> in place of the king who wielded his omnipotence
> without control or limit in the privacy of his palace,
> Greek political life aimed to become the subject of
> public debate, in the broad daylight of the agora,
> between citizens who were defined as equals and for
> whom the state was the common undertaking ... [A]
> new thought sought to base the order of the world
> on relations of symmetry, equilibrium, and equality
> among the various elements that made up the
> cosmos.[67]

Party conflict – which eventually the Romans tried, but ultimately failed, to resolve with the structure of the "republic" – was an inevitable part of this process. Vernant notes that "this equilibrium of forces was by no means static; it encompassed opposition, it was formed out of conflict."[68] The idea of democracy led to the idea of a distributed and centerless vision of the universe – the new social cosmos leading to a new way of reading the physical cosmos: "It was the equality and symmetry of the various powers that made up the cosmos that characterized the new natural order … *Monarchia* was replaced, in nature as in the city, by a rule of *isonomia*."[69]

Democracy's "regulatory" function was thus to declare a fundamental *isonomia* (equality) as the heart of social relations – an entirely new idea. But this was an equality that sought a rhythmic patterning for, rather than strict leveling of, social differences – one in which balance would be kept by maintaining an absence at the social center – the empty space of the agora, the blindness of the law, in which all participated equally and before which all were equals. By Vernant's account, "under the yoke of a *dike* that is the same for all, the elementary forces are connected and coordinated in a regular rhythm, so that despite their multiplicity and diversity, they form a single cosmos."[70]

When the center becomes inhabited by the influence of some particular element of the social whole, when material (financial) and social inequalities are allowed to develop to the point at which they shape and indeed determine what transpires in the agora and the law, democracy as such ceases. What democracy ought to enable in the face of this problem, but for which it has yet to develop the adequate mechanism, is recalibrating the rhythm that balances the social *isonomia* when it inevitably goes out of equilibrium. Democracy ought to find methods of adaptation to its own processes of change management. Experiments with direct democracy, as employed in the Occupy movement, are just such attempts to increase democracy's self-regulatory abilities.

Such rewritten social rhythms are exactly what the Invisible Committee is talking about when they note that "revolutionary movements do not spread by contamination but by resonance."[71] Democracies – where they can exist at all – are, basically, slowly unfolding, permanent revolutions. They "regulate" the social sphere via a slow but constant revolution.

In more or less traditional Marxist terms, **changes in the material base of production and social relations condition (but do not determine) changes in the superstructure of culture and ideology.**

In *The Communist Manifesto*, Marx asks, "Does it require deep insight to comprehend that people's ideas, views, and conceptions – in a word, their consciousness – changes with their conditions of existence, their social relations, and their life in society?"[72] David Harvey problematizes Marx's position when he asks: if consciousness is determined by material relations of production, how then is it even possible to critique capitalism, and offer alternatives to it, if that critique and those alternatives are themselves determined by the existing structure of capitalism?

> Marx's historical materialism has a problem in preparing our imaginations (let alone our political practices) for the creation of a socialist (or for that matter any other) alternative … The historical-geographical experience of revolutionary movements in power (and of materialized utopianism of any sort) indicates the deep seriousness of the problem of unpreparedness for radical change. Many revolutionary movements did not or could not free themselves from ways of thinking embedded in the material circumstances of their past.[73]

It's in light of this that movements focusing on developing new modes of social relations and new, egalitarian forms of self-governance, building the new society within the shell of the old, are perhaps at an advantage. This is to invest in imaginative experimentation simultaneously at the level of production and social relations, and at the level of ideas, "meaning," art and yes, even consciousness. We have seen this in the Occupy movement, with its focus on the distribution of food, medicine, the provision of shelter, and in new (for most participants) social practices such as the consensus-based general assembly, working groups, and their extensive educational and cultural programs ("consciousness raising").

Crucial, though, is the fact that the material base does not *determine* the ideological superstructure, but rather, *conditions* it – which is an important difference. Setting the circumstances in which ideologies will evolve is not the same thing as determining the outcomes and substance of ideologies and thought. Indeed, evolutionary biology and cultural evolution, as I have touched on them here, suggest that a certain degree of randomness, chance, and unpredictable, imaginative *leaping* is built into the "conditions" of life and thus the dynamics of evolutionary change. Our very *overdetermination* by a complex matrix of forces paradoxically leaves room for our freedom.

Everywhere the poverty of thought around alternatives to capitalism has been noted and either lamented or celebrated. "Utopia" became a bad word – the market seemed to usurp its very language – and it became easier to imagine the end of the world in some natural (or intergalactic) cataclysm than to imagine a world without capitalism. But, as Alain Badiou argues in *The Communist Hypothesis*, broad social change requires a vision of another world – as well as the sense that such social changes at the systemic level are even possible. For Badiou, "in order to anticipate, at least ideologically, or intellectually, the creation of new possibilities, we must have an Idea … an Idea that also involves the formal possibility of *other* possibilities, ones as yet unsuspected by us. An Idea is always the assertion that a new truth is historically possible."[74]

Being "anti-capitalist" is not enough. We need to know what the *absence* of capitalism would be like, to see how we might live there. Part of what needs to be imagined, then, is *what* we might change into – but we also need guides as to *how* we will bring about such a change. To engage our agency in the process of social change is in part to take on much needed "imaginative" work, as well as equally imaginative "activist" experimentation with forms of "demonstration" and new forms of social organization. We must explore and extrapolate the idea whose time has come. As Harvey notes, "There is a time and a place in the ceaseless human endeavor to change the world, when alternative visions, no matter how fantastic, provide the grist for shaping powerful political forces for change."[75]

Harvey's *Spaces of Hope* is a virtual manual for social change. I can do little better than to continue quoting him at length.

> Any contemporary struggle to envision a reconstruction of the social process has to confront the problem of how to overthrow the structures (both physical and institutional) that the free market has itself produced as relatively permanent features of our world. Though daunting, the task is not impossible. The revolutionary agenda of neoliberalism has accomplished a lot in the way of physical and institutional change these last twenty years ... So why, then, can we not envision equally dramatic changes (though pointing in a different direction) as we seek for alternatives? ... Only by changing our institutional world can we change ourselves at the same time, as it is only through the desire to change ourselves that institutional change can occur.[76]

★

May 1

THESIS 12

Although it has become something of a postmodern cliché, **when it comes to revolution**, in terms of opening moves at least, **the medium really is the message.**

Slavoj Žižec, writing about the 2005 suburban Paris riots, argues, "What is most difficult to accept is precisely the riots' meaninglessness" – that they were "an impulsive movement into action which can't be translated into speech or thought and carries with it an intolerable weight of frustration."[77]

I propose this same analysis be applied to the riots in London and Vancouver in the summer of 2011 – these conflagrations were preludes in many ways, like the austerity riots in Greece, to the more "strategic" and speech-intensive moves of the fall occupations that followed. Revolutionary change begins with the social "boiling over" (such metaphors are typical) of frustrations. The point of spontaneous street demonstrations and riots – if we can speak in terms of a "point" here – is simply to signal that something is deeply wrong, something which can no longer be tolerated. "The [2005 Paris] riots were simply a direct effort to gain visibility," Žižec writes, and "their aim was to create a problem, to signal that they [the rioters] were a problem that could no longer be ignored."[78]

Part of the "point" of revolutions, then – part of their process, the means by which they typically *begin* – is to signal, at a basic and fundamental level, that everyone is *not* in agreement with the status quo, that a sizeable constituency will no longer tolerate current social relations, and that "things must change." Insurrection and revolt – including rioting and the simple refusal to continue in one's established social role – are such means of deep, overpowering social expression. They are not the result of "a few bad apples," but the commons' own deepest dissatisfaction boiling over, indignant and enraged. When more than 250,000 people take to Montreal's streets, as they have in March and May 2012, the message is, quite literally, *this is what democracy looks like*. If we are indeed going to have a democracy, we had better be able to pay real attention to this groundswell of discontent and indignation arising in the commons.

Hannah Arendt, in her classic *On Revolution*, also addresses the "problem of beginning" when she posits that "revolutions are the only political events which confront us directly and inevitably with the problem of beginning" – for they "are not mere changes ... Antiquity was well acquainted with political change and the violence that went with change, but neither of them appeared to it to bring about something altogether new."[79]

If we are to imagine revolutions as resetting the clocks, and indeed initiating "something altogether new," then they *are* as much about the very self-creating act of "breaking out," "breaking with," and "breaking free" as they are anything else. Seen from this vantage point, Arendt's dictum that "revolutions ... are not even conceivable outside the domain of violence"[80] appears to be fatefully true: they involve "breaking," and thus at a primary level are about signaling the very need for and act of "breaking" some existing structure or formation. They are acts of social pointing, phatic expressions which let the world know, "*We are here!*"

However, as Arendt notes "concern with stability" and "the spirit of the new" "have become opposites in political thought and terminology," despite the fact that this does not have to be so, and the fact that they were indeed "not mutually exclusive opposites but two sides of the same event" at the time of the French Revolution. "Terminologically speaking, the effort to recapture the lost spirit of revolution must, to a certain extent, consist in the attempt at thinking together and combining meaningfully what our present vocabulary presents to us in terms of opposition and contradiction."[81] This "thinking together" can be figured in a merger of medium and message, but it also turns our attention to the very substance of the changes we try to institute in society.

I have argued as much already about the Occupy movement: its strength and true potentiality derive from sidestepping such either/or polarizing debates as that old, artificial choice between reform and revolution. In Arendt's terms, we can both work toward a reformation of what currently passes for "stability" (the existing system, in certain aspects) as we simultaneously work on the "new" society that will ultimately "replace" the existing order (the engineering of which requires time). The acceptance and choice to work with the dynamic energy of such contradictions is at the very heart of social transformation today, brought about by the urgency of a rapidly changing world (requiring the differential time-scales for both short-term "reforms" and long-term "revolutions" in the present structure).

But to return to the medium-as-message question, a social formation that Arendt locates at the origin of revolutions is also very much part and parcel of the content and substance of the changed world that revolutions try to bring into being. Arendt here has in mind the "revolutionary societies" and the system of autonomous "wards" of the French and American Revolutions – "elementary republics" that "sprang up as the spontaneous organs of the people." These formations proffered "an entirely new form of government, with a new public space for freedom which was constituted and organized during the course of the revolution itself."[82] The very language Robespierre employed looks ahead to later movements also based upon "assemblies where the citizens [could] occupy themselves in common with these [public] matters."[83]

Virtually all revolutions begin with the spontaneous appearance of small, local, grass-roots assemblies and "councils" formed to take over some (ideally all) of the processes of communal self-organization – in response either to the collapse (imminent or actual) or egregious dysfunction of the centralized governmental apparatus of the State. Arendt writes:

> Outstanding among the council's common charac-
> teristics is, of course, the spontaneity of their coming
> into being, because it clearly and flagrantly contra-
> dicts the theoretical "twentieth century model of
> revolution – planned, prepared, and executed almost

to cold scientific exactness by the professional revolutionaries."[84]

Nevertheless, the history of revolutions shows how those "professional" or professionalizing revolutionaries – often on the basis of arguments for expediency and pragmatism – betrayed the horizontal, decentralized revolutionary spirit, refusing to accept the message of the medium. Arendt observes that

> the councils, obviously, were spaces of freedom. As such, they inevitably refused to regard themselves as temporary organs of revolution and, on the contrary, made all attempts at establishing themselves as permanent organs of government … It was nothing more or less than this hope of a transformation of the state, for a new form of government that would permit every member of the modern egalitarian society to become a 'participator' in public affairs, that was buried in the disasters of twentieth-century revolutions.[85]

Learning from the revolutionary past, and trying not to fall into the same traps, is of course crucial. We also have to remember that revolutions are by their very nature *about* the future, about altered mediums and their concomitant messages that might produce a social difference to come. What's being signaled today is less about present conditions (though they are often terrible, and definitely worsening) than about the prospect of future conditions. The students demonstrating in Quebec as I write this are resisting a future of indebtedness. In an economy increasingly dependent upon massive levels of personal debt, such a revolt can only be presented in the existing order as an appalling rending of the entire social fabric; these student revolutionaries appear nothing less than selfish ingrates who have the gall to refuse their destined future of debt servitude. How dare they!

The key things we may take from past revolutions are the hope and possibility of radical change. Revolutions are revolutionary to the extent that they declare, *"This can happen. Radical change is both real and possible.* Another world is possible." It is the psychic space revolution opens that matters – the imaginary it sets loose through its very medium.

THESIS 13

Debt drives capitalism's manic pursuit of growth, and keeps us chained to the wheel.

Without getting too deep into the psychology of why people generally do not embrace, and in fact actively resist, change – even when it is patently in their own long-term best interests (that because there is so much change all around us, all the time, establishing the very essence of our daily lives, we attempt to create and maintain artificial "bubbles" of changelessness?) – we can see a good deal of compulsion and blatant shortsightedness in our economic practices and structures.

We return here to David Harvey's problem "of how to overthrow the structures (both physical and institutional) that the free market has itself produced." One of the reasons capitalism is so difficult to shift as a system (aside from the issue of sheer scale, of the gravity of power imbalances), so paradoxically protean and sclerotic, changeable on a daily basis and yet resistant to attempts to change it structurally, over larger time scales, is the way it has been built and how it has increasingly come to depend upon interest-bearing debt. Debt causes constant transformation and exchanges of wealth, but despite its busy surface, it does not change structurally; in fact it builds the maintenance of its structure into its daily operations. Like capitalism itself, debt both constantly changes, and never changes. It is, in many respects, the ultimate expression of the ancient Greek idea of "rest in change" – of a sort of stability formed from constant movement.[86] Or so it is hoped and projected, packaged and sold (until a bubble bursts and a collapse occurs). Debt thus also powers the constant need to grow (in order to service one's debt and to accumulate surplus profit from investment above and beyond this) that so characterizes capitalism.

As Charles Eisenstein notes, at the heart of the problem lies "how money is created: as interest-bearing debt."

> At any moment, because of interest, the amount of money in existence is always less than the amount of debt. The only way to avoid defaults, unemployment and concentration of wealth is for new money to be constantly created through further lending. Lending can only happen and loans can only be repaid when there are profitable investment opportunities: the creation of new goods and services. That is, it can only happen in the presence of economic growth. When the economy stops growing, debt rises faster than income, defaults rise, employment falls, and the concentration of wealth intensifies.
>
> To prevent this, politicians across the political spectrum seek economic growth. Ideally, if the economy grows fast enough, the owners of wealth can keep getting richer by lending money at interest – and the borrowers can get richer too, by increasing their revenues faster than the rate of interest. That plan worked pretty well in the 1950s and 1960s, but today it is becoming increasingly apparent that the planet cannot accommodate much more economic growth. As the growth rate has slowed, economic inequality has increased. For a time the developed world "imported growth" by stripping natural resources and social capital from nations that still had a lot of it. Today, though, these sources of growth are running out as well. We are left with the dregs of the barrel: for example, the Alberta Tar Sands.[87]

Eisenstein succinctly summarizes the process by which interest-bearing debt chains our economies to the wheel of growth – and how this is in turn linked to resource extraction and environmental destruction. David Graeber, in his recent study of debt, offers us a clear picture of both its origins and the way in which its promotion is used to keep us, quite literally, *invested in*, and *indebted to*, capitalism as an economic system. The former is, like Marx once noted, a story written "in letters of blood and fire"[88]: interest-bearing debts funded wars, expansion, and colonial conquest, which in turn drove a system of debt servitude (the lowest and poorest would have to pay for the excesses of the wealthy and grand) and spurred nascent capitalists on to even further extremes of violence and repression (colonization, enclosure, industrialization) in the manic urge to service debts and extract profits beyond the interest owed.

> [W]hat we see at the dawn of modern capitalism is a gigantic financial apparatus of credit and debt that operates – in practical effect – to pump more and more labor out of just about everyone with whom it comes into contact, and as a result produces an endlessly expanding volume of material goods. It does so not just by moral compulsion, but above all by using moral compulsion to mobilize sheer physical forces.[89]

"War, conquest, and slavery," Graeber continues, "played the central role in converting human economies into market ones," and "Any system that reduces the world to numbers can only be held in place by weapons."[90] But later periods in capitalism's evolution found better methods for maintaining its seemingly unsustainable marriage of the "gambler" and the "financier."[91]

> By the end of World War II, the specter of an imminent working-class uprising that had so haunted the ruling classes of Europe and North America for the previous century had largely disappeared. To put it crudely: the white working class of the North Atlantic countries, from the United States to West Germany, were offered a deal. If they agreed to set aside any fantasies of fundamentally changing the nature of the system, then they would be allowed to keep their unions, enjoy a wide variety of social benefits (pensions, vacations, health care …), and,

perhaps most important, through generously funded
and ever-expanding public educational institutions,
know that their children had a reasonable chance of
leaving the working class entirely.[92]

This was the "Keynesian" system that held for the first thirty
or so years after the war. Then, over the next thirty years (from
the mid-1970s to the present, more or less) this "social safety net"
was eroded and largely replaced with a *new* "new deal." "In the
new dispensation," Graeber argues, "wages would no longer rise,
but workers were encouraged to buy a piece of capitalism" – and
thus become not the system's adversaries, nor its bribed
participants, but its indebted "investors," wholly dependent upon
its continued growth.[93] Pensions were invested in the market, and
everyone was encouraged to "play the market" in whatever way
they could. Everyone was encouraged to borrow, and credit cards,
with their ever-expanding "limits," were offered to all and sundry,
new applications seeming to arrive daily in the mail. As housing
prices went through the roof, everyone was encouraged to take
out larger and larger mortgages, which were made available at ever
lower interest rates, even to borrowers once deemed too risky to
qualify for financing of any kind. Now, almost every one of us is
in debt – tied to a market system in which our very indebtedness
has made us interested parties.

How hard is it to change the system upon which one's hopes –
fleeting as they may be – are pegged? How hard is it to find the
time and energy to criticize or even protest the system that keeps
one running as fast as one can in a breathless pursuit of solvency?
This is the trap so many of us now find ourselves in – a trap, one
has to assume, carefully set and sprung by those who are *truly*
heavily invested in their power and privilege, but who are set up,
as Graeber makes clear, to stay well ahead of the suffering majority
in the tail-chasing game of debt.

What is the solution? "To begin to free ourselves," Graeber
suggests, "the first thing we need to do is to see ourselves as
historical actors, as people who can make a difference in the
course of world events. This is exactly what the militarization of
history is trying to take away."[94] Easier said than done, no doubt.

More than this though, we need to recall that powerful mechanisms like debt and interest are the creations of historical social forces – made, and thus open to being *unmade*, by us. If capitalism teaches anything, it is that human beings have the power to set world-altering forces in motion. The speed and relative ease with which governments could erase the debts of banks judged "too big to fail" places another possibility on the table: erasing the debts of the commons, erasing the very idea of fiscal indebtedness – a jubilee for a species and a planet that we must, if there is to be any hope at all, consider "too big to fail." Such a jubilee will not be granted by the bankers and political leaders currently running the debt show. Such a jubilee also goes by another name – revolution. We can only grant it ourselves.

★

Paul Klee
Angelus Novus, 1920

THESIS 14 - CODA

A Klee painting named "Angelus Novus"
shows an angel looking as though he is about
to move away from something he is fixedly
contemplating. His eyes are staring, his
mouth is open, his wings are spread. This is
how one pictures the angel of history. His face
is turned towards the past. Where we perceive
a chain of events, he sees one single
catastrophe which keeps piling wreckage
upon wreckage and hurls it in front of his feet.
The angel would like to stay, awaken the dead,
and make whole what has been smashed. But
a storm is blowing from Paradise; it has got
caught in his wings with such violence that
the angel can no longer close them. This
storm irresistibly propels him into the future
to which his back is turned, while the pile of
debris before him grows skyward. This storm
is what we call progress.

> – WALTER BENJAMIN
> "Theses on the Philosophy of History"

Our society at large, and our elected and unelected "leaders"
especially, are ignoring the wider crisis we are in the midst of.
From hollow consumerism to growing inequality to mass suffering
and ecocide, we will not look at the mounting pile of wreckage,
but, instead, speed on with our self-destructive plunder of the
planet. Those who do look – who find the wreckage and are unable
to tear their eyes away – are angels of history. Those who go a step
further and find themselves struggling against the storm, who try

to wake the dead and make whole what has been shattered – these are angels of change, the activists and workaday people who refuse to do nothing and find themselves in the streets.

Where is the lever, I've wondered, the switch we can grasp and pull this screaming machine to a grinding halt? That's what the people occupying squares all over the world are demanding, "*Where's the lever?*" Time to give it a pull.

No *one* can grasp our culture whole now – it has become far too complex for that – no *one* can pull the lever. The effort – as ever – must be collective and cumulative. But it must be swift and broad-based, too. This is why the spontaneity and the "99%" rhetoric of Occupy are so important. We must act now, we must act together – all our futures are dependent upon this fundamental change history now requires – if it is to continue to unfold. What we need is agency and imagination. These are already part of our patrimony as human beings.

Admittedly, democracy – that name for a system in which the people actually organize themselves, for their own collective benefit – is incredibly difficult and complex to manage at any considerable scale. Centralized, elite, minority rule is *easy* and often "efficient." Which is why we have relied on it in one way, shape, or form for much of recorded history (keeping in mind that what we now call "democracies" are so in name only, masking the reality of an elite plutocracy). As a species we, like all others, tend to be as dumb as we can get away with being – thus conserving valuable energy. To have real democracy, we need help – we need a mechanism, a process that minimizes how taxing such a system can be (thus making the corner-cutting of elite rule less attractive), as well as an education system designed to produce critical, democratic thinkers. New political ideas are called for, new experiments in social relations conducted. If the tendency of systems is toward increasing complexity, we should be capable of democracy.

Our debt-driven economy requires perpetual growth, which contradicts the second law of thermodynamics – that is, we are driven by an impossibility we will fail to fulfill. Our economy must be entirely rebuilt and refounded – on the basis not of debt and growth, but on the basis of the maintenance of the gifts of the commons. To do this, to make this change, we need to wrest the political system from those who now control it and benefit from the economy of debt and growth – we must grasp the mechanism and process of a true democracy, which is a government by the commons, for the commons. This now needs to be an expanded commons including all species, and it needs to be based upon transgenerational thinking. As Clive Ponting states bluntly, "Human societies have rarely taken account of anything except short-term considerations."[95] This has to change, now.

It's strange, perhaps, to wind up thinking about the future in the middle of Rome. But Rome is as much – perhaps more – of a reminder of how things have gone wrong, as it is a springboard in history to leap once more toward the possibility of real democracy tomorrow. The "natural cycle" of modes of government found in Aristotle, Polybius, and Rousseau, and thus throughout the Western philosophy of politics, is more accurately a perpetual dialectic of minority and mass, centralization and decentralization, the 1% and the 99%. Democracy is about the use of such dialectics to erase once and for all the disequilibrium that confounds us. We, the people of this world, are finding each other. But we are also locating our enemies – the structures that perpetuate them, the places where they operate the levers of exploitation.

In Rome, on October 15, 2011, the attempt to occupy the Piazza San Giovanni devolved into what the media simply referred to as "violence." There were perhaps two hundred thousand people marching. But there was also, along the route, a riot, and a pitched battle with the police. As one report suggested, behind the supposed "ugliness" that prevented the occupation of Rome there is another "'ugly' story to be told" – a story "of a generation of Italian young people that has no jobs and perceives to have no future; a generation of young people who are not just 'indignant' – they are bitter, resentful, and angry at a system that does not represent them."[96]

Rome, I have come to think, both its past and its present, shows us the "ugliness" of the rage felt by so many who are excluded and exploited, as well as the closely related ugliness of the police state ready to meet this indignation with violent repression, and the ugliness of governments ready, in the first place, to sacrifice all for the continued growth and accumulation of the wealth of the privileged elite. But amid ugliness, we may yet find beauty. Rummaging in the past, we might find the spring-boards and building blocks of new, as yet unrealized futures.

Reading back over this essay, I see the word "inevitable" on many of its pages. One thing the history of change teaches is that the "inevitable" is largely a historical construct – that many things that once seemed inevitable have come, in the course of time, to in fact be *evitable*.[97] Pursuing change, we are in fact pursuing a process of making the inevitable evitable. If I have argued that change, whether biological or social, is inevitable – that it is, fundamentally, what is – I would only add that within the large patters of evolutionary and historical inevitability there is always the potential for many local *evitabilities*. This is where we may act as social agents – this is where we gather and facilitate change together.

The question isn't just, "*How do we change the world?*" It's, "*How do we live in a perpetually changing world – how do we live a life that is oriented toward change? How do we live so that a changed world is ever and always possible? How do we live within the possibility of change, the possibility of possibility, the law that tomorrow will need to change again?*"

We are protean change producers and change managers. We must now, more than ever, engage our collective agency to produce the sorts of changes that avoid global harms and manage the enormous changes wrought by our past and present collective activities. We must all become revolutionaries. We must all assemble, protest, and demonstrate, creatively willing a new world from the shell of the old.

In Quebec this spring, as thousands gather to bang their pots and pans in nightly "casseroles," this is exactly what is afoot once again. I can think of no better way of concluding than with the words of Montreal resident and rabble.ca correspondent Ethan Cox: "This is what keeps the powerful awake at night. If we talk, if we exchange ideas and debate the future of our society, we will want to change it. And nothing terrifies the powerful more than a change to the system which gives them their power."[98]

Notes

Preface

1   There are obvious differences between the Vancouver and London riots – different instigating circumstances, and different social circumstances in the two cities. However, both drew the ire of politicians and many media pundits who saw them as the meaningless response of a spoiled and entitled generation with nothing better to do. In fact, the socioeconomic situations in the two cities – again, though different – have more to say about their "causes." To cite just one Canadian explanation that seems to me to be nearest the mark, Adrian Mack and Miranda Nelson, writing in the *Georgia Straight*, note: "In reality, matters have only gotten much worse politically and economically since 1994, and Generation Y has been delivered into a beyond-callous world facing a perfect storm of crises. They know it. What does the future look like for the average 20 year old? It's a depressing, empty place where they can't get decent-paying (let alone secure) jobs or ever have a hope of owning property. Can you imagine how much more fearful and angry they would be if they fully comprehended the seriousness of peak oil?" See "Vancouver Hockey Riot Is a Symptom of a Larger Problem," June 16, 2011, http://www.straight.com/article-399635/vancouver/vancouver-hockey-riot-symptom-larger-problem.

2   The media committee had many failings, however it managed to produce a regular blog, some excellent videos (the work of Ian MacKenzie and Jordan Boschman is exemplary here), and a fairly reliable livestream (I note the dedication of Cameron Bode and Courtenay Harrop in this regard).

3   Hannah Arendt, *On Revolution* (New York: Viking Press, 1963), 246.

4   Fredric Jameson, *Archaeologies of the Future: The Desire Called Utopia and Other Science Fictions* (London: Verso, 2005), xii–xiii.

5   See for instance Harsha Walia's excellent "Letter to Occupy Together Movement," published on rabble.ca on October 14, 2011, in which

she argues that the name "Occupy" "has a deeply colonialist implication." Walia also notes that the movement has so far been "brilliantly transitional." I write in the hope that it indeed remains so, and that the question of its proper name is itself still in transition.

6 Translating the printemps erable [collective], "An Open Letter to the Mainstream English Media," www.quebecprotest.com, May 24, 2012, http://www.quebecprotest.com/post/23754797322/an-open-letter-to-the-mainstream-english-media.

Part 1
Repetition and Difference: Occupying the History of Change

1 David Meslin, "Redefining Apathy" (lecture, TEDx, Toronto, October 9, 2010).

2 *Globe and Mail*, January 29, 2011, A10–11.

3 This is a complex issue, but it involves changes in the media since 9/11 (for example, the media's general willingness to ignore dissenting voices and uncritically accept government positions) and the "criminalization of dissent," as it is often called, enabled by legislative changes such as the USA PATRIOT Act. See, for instance, Jules Boykoff, *The Suppression of Dissent: How the State and Mass Media Squelch USAmerican Social Movements* (London: Routledge, 2006).

4 Henri Lefebvre, *The Explosion: Marxism and the French Revolution*, trans. Alfred Ehrenfeld (New York: Monthly Review Press, 1969), 7.

5 Alain Badiou argues that "we are the contemporaries of '68" still. See *The Communist Hypothesis* (London: Verso, 2010).

6 Ibid., 30.

7 Ibid., 57–58.

8 The 2012 Quebec Student strikes are the longest running and most extensive in Canadian history. They have also produced the largest mass demonstrations in Canadian history, with several hundred thousand people in the Montreal streets on March 22, April 22, and May 22, 2012). In May the movement began to spread across the country and around the world, with solidarity marches in hundreds of other cities.

9 Lefebvre, *Explosion*, 60–61.

10 Ibid., 62.

11 The Invisible Committee, *The Coming Insurrection* (Los Angeles: Semiotext(e), 2009), 14.

12 Lefebvre, *Explosion*, 70–72.

13 Ibid., 82.

14 The Invisible Committee, *The Coming Insurrection*, 96.

15 Lefebvre, *Explosion*, 89.

16 Ibid., 113.

17 The Invisible Committee, *The Coming Insurrection*, 113–17.

18 The constant presence of insurrectionary possibility was also indicated by the arsenal of signs that came to visually mark each occupation – at the ready for spontaneous marches, with slogans and messages tailored to a range of issues and contexts.

19 Lefebvre, *Explosion*, 12.

20 Ibid., 115.

21 The Invisible Committee, *The Coming Insurrection*, 122.

22 Ibid., 14.

23 David Graeber, "Concerning the Violent Peace Police: An Open Letter to Chris Hedges," published widely on the Internet, February 9, 2012.

24 Chris Hedges, "The Cancer in Occupy," truthdig, February 6, 2012, http://www.truthdig.com/report/item/the_cancer_of_occupy_2012 0206/.

25 Zakk Flash, "Hedging Our Bets on the Black Bloc: The Impotence of Mere Liberalism," Infoshop, February 7, 2012, http://news.info shop.org/article.php?story=20120207100008741.

26 It should be noted that "diversity of tactics" does not simply mean doing whatever you want. It implies tactics, differently employed by different groups. One masked and black-clad militant running off from a peaceful march to challenge the police is not an example of diverse tactics. But a group of twenty masked and black-clad militants doing so might be.

27 Graeber, "Concerning the Violent Peace Police."

28 Attributed to Alice Walker and in wide circulation via social media throughout the fall of 2011.

29 Herbert Haines, *Black Radicals and the Civil Rights Mainstream, 1954–1970* (Knoxville: University of Tennessee Press, 1988), 5.

30 Haines, *Black Radicals*, 2.

31 Ibid., 184. It's been noted that there's a difference between the diverse tactics of distinct groups (the Southern Christian Leadership Conference and the Black Panthers) and a diversity of tactics within a single group. However, with a global movement like Occupy, this distinction breaks down, and solidarity across a range of movement formations becomes even more necessary.

32 "Revolutions … are not even conceivable outside the domain of violence" (*On Revolution*, 18).

33 There were always inherent differences between those who camped at the VAG and those who did not. The campers, for one thing, dealt more directly with, and were in part composed of, marginalized people (the homeless, addicts). Tent City reported to the GA, much like any other committee or working group; eventually, however, it came to see itself as an autonomous body not beholden to the GA.

34 A young man was discovered unconscious and not breathing in his tent early on Thursday, November 3, 2011. Occupy Vancouver medic Mathew Kagis was the first to treat the victim, who was subsequently revived by paramedics. For a report see the *Vancouver Courier* (http://www.vancourier.com/Occupy+Vancouver+first +volunteer+describes+overdose+drama/5659074/story.html). Details about the second, fatal overdose can be found in the relevant "Dispatches" entries, "Tragedy on the Commons" and "Turning Tides and Sacred Fires."

35 The corporate-sponsored CIBC LunarFest, which occupied the VAG grounds just a few months after Occupy Vancouver, had propane tanks and cooking facilities inside tents, and went unmolested by the fire department.

36 Young white men oblivious to their privilege, and the subsequent alienation of many women within the movement, have probably been Occupy's biggest failing. Patriarchy has been a pillar of exploitation and oppression as long as there has been exploitation and oppression, so it's no surprise that this fundamental "inequality" has been the hardest to eradicate from the movement, and the first to come racing back into the vacuum of the potential "new society" under construction. Clearly, if the movement is to go forward effectively, it must first and foremost deal directly with male privilege and the marginalization and intimidation of women.

37 OWS organizer Marisa Holmes, speaking in Vancouver in June 2012, noted that the movement "brought anarchism into popular culture."

38 Lefebvre, *Explosion*, 122.

39 Ibid., 126.

40 Richard J.F. Day, *Gramsci Is Dead: Anarchist Currents in the Newest Social Movements*, (London: Pluto Press / Toronto: Between the Lines, 2005), 7–8.

41 Ibid., 8.

42 Ibid., 14–15.

43 Ibid., 10.

44 David Graeber, "The New Anarchists," *New Left Review* 13 (January–February 2002).

45 David Graeber, *Direct Action – An Ethnography* (Oakland: AK Press, 2009), 527.

46 Ibid., 203, 528.

47 Ibid., 530.

48 Ibid., 532.

49 Those who question this could do no better than heed a recent study posted on businessinsider.com, "Corporate Profits Just Hit an All-Time High, Wages Just Hit an All-Time Low." With these statistics coming amid the continuing push for austerity measures, corporate tax breaks, and deregulation, it's difficult to argue that we aren't living under a system of "corporate welfare."

50 Day, *Gramsci is Dead*, 95. Another way of gesturing toward the nebulous nature of this indescribable enemy is found in Michael Hardt and Antonio Negri's ubiquitous, but slippery, *Empire* (Cambridge: Harvard University Press, 2000), xii.: "In contrast to imperialism, *Empire* establishes no territorial center of power and does not rely on fixed boundaries or barriers. It is a decentered and deterritorializing apparatus of rule that progressively incorporates the entire global realm within its open, expanding frontiers."

51 Jodi Dean, "Claiming Division, Naming a Wrong," in *Occupy! Scenes from Occupied America*, ed. Astra Taylor, Keith Gessen, et al (London: Verso Books, 2011), 88.

52 #HowToCamp, quoted in Sarah van Gelder, ed., *This Changes Everything: Occupy Wall Street and the 99% Movement* (San Francisco: BK Publishers, 2011) 1.

53 Slavoj Žižec, "Don't Fall in Love with Yourselves" in *Occupy! Scenes from Occupied America*, 68.

54 The SOPA bill (Stop Online Piracy Act) in the United States is seen by its critics to sacrifice free speech in the name of extending online private property rights, while in Canada Bill C-30 ("Investigating and Preventing Criminal Electronic Communications Act") would give authorities unprecedented access to Internet users' information without a warrant. While neither of these pieces of legislation is directly aimed at reducing activists' ability to organize online, they are certainly examples of government attempts to regulate, delimit, and enclose the burgeoning commons of the Internet.

55 The National Defense Authorization Act, while still in legal and constitutional limbo, was rushed into law on New Year's Eve, 2011. Section 1021 of the law appears to grant the president the power to detain US citizens without charge or trial. Bill C-78 was enacted on May 18, 2012, in response to the ongoing student strike in Quebec. It imposes extensive restrictions on the freedoms of association,

assembly, and expression. Bill C-38, Canada's omnibus budget bill, could also be considered in this context; it includes legislation aimed directly at reducing environmental organizations' access to the environmental review process, and calls their funding into question.

56 Quoted in Graeber, "The New Anarchists."
57 See Naomi Klein, *The Shock Doctrine: The Rise of Disaster Capitalism* (Toronto: Vintage Canada, 2008), 5–7.
58 The Invisible Committee, *The Coming Insurrection*, 63, 80.
59 Lefebvre, *Explosion*, 122.

Part 2
Dispatches from the Occupation

1 Michael Kimmelman, "In Protest, the Power of Place," New York Times Sunday Review, October 15, 2011.
2 Henry David Thoreau, "Resistance to Civil Government," in *Walden and Resistance to Civil Government*, ed. William Rossi (New York: Norton, 1966), 245.
3 The preamble to the IWW constitution, written in 1905, can still be found on their website, www.iww.org.
4 The 5:00 a.m. raid on the Occupy Oakland encampment was widely covered in the media and watched via Livestream by many activists around the world. See, for example, Occupy Oakland's own coverage: http://occupyoakland.org/2011/10/police-brutalize-dismantle-occupy-oakland-camp/.
5 Wolfgang Streeck, "The Crises of Democratic Capitalism," *New Left Review* 71 (September–October, 2011): 5–29
6 See, for instance, Toby Sanger, "Don't Just Occupy Wall Street, Tax It," *Toronto Star*, October 12, 2011, http://www.thestar.com/ opinion/editorialopinion/article/1068681--don-t-just-occupy-wall-street-tax-it.
7 Žižec, "Don't Fall in Love with Yourselves," 68.
8 David Harvey, "The Right to the City," *New Left Review* 53 (September–October 2008): 23.
9 David Harvey, "The Party of Wall Street Meets Its Nemesis" *Verso Books* (blog), October 28, 2011.
10 For many years, women – often sex-trade workers – have disappeared from Vancouver's Downtown Eastside, a neighborhood rocked by poverty, drugs, and neglect – but also long the seat of community activism. Many of the women, a striking majority of them First Nations, were the victims of serial killer Robert Pickton.

Many feel that the Vancouver Police Department and the RCMP ignored signs that a serial killer was active in the neighborhood, and botched the subsequent investigation. An inquiry into the handling of the case was underway during the period of the Occupy Vancouver encampment.

11 The cause of death was indeed later reported to be a drug overdose. A small consolation is that this incident sparked debates about "drug policy" and the eventual adoption of a "harm reduction" strategy at the camp – something that the dozens of yearly overdose deaths in the city of Vancouver rarely do.

12 Bill Tieleman, "Occupy Vancouver a Sad Parody of Revolution," *24 Hours*, November 8, 2011, http://vancouver.24hrs.ca/Columnists/ NewsViewsAttitude/2011/11/07/18936791.html.

13 Michael Stone, "How the Occupy Movement Can Deal with Conflict" (lecture, Occupy Vancouver, November 6, 2011).

14 Chu's comments were reported in many newspapers. See Jeff Lee and Doug Ward, "Goodwill Gone at Occupy Vancouver: VPD Chief," *Vancouver Sun*, November 9, 2011, http://www.vancouver-sun.com/news/Goodwill+gone+Occupy+Vancouver+chief/567643 5/story.html.

15 Michael Stewart, "In Vancouver, Occupy Was Already Alienated," *Rabble*, November 10, 2011, http://rabble.ca/blogs/bloggers/michael -stewart/2011/11/vancouver-occupy-was-already-alienated.

16 Geoff Olson, "View Occupy Vancouver as Global Symptom not Local Blight," *Vancouver Courier*, November 10, 2011, http://www .vancourier.com/View+Occupy+Vancouver+global+symptom+loc al+blight/5691133/story.html.

17 Widely reported. See for instance Jim Gold, "Mayors Deny Colluding on 'Occupy' Crackdowns," msnbc.com, November 15, 2011. Rumors have surfaced that there may also have been co-ordination with federal governments behind the scenes.

18 Luc Boltanski and Eve Chiapello, *The New Spirit of Capitalism*, trans. Gregory Elliott (London: Verso, 2005), 22.

19 The City of Vancouver sought and was granted an injunction to evict the Occupy Vancouver encampment. This meant that defiance of the injunction would carry a charge of contempt of court – a more serious charge than mere bylaw infraction. A decision was made to move the encampment, but after two failed attempts to do so, the camp was disbanded. Exhaustion and frustration probably played as large a role in the camp's demise as court orders and po-lice enforcement. No activists were satisfied with the final outcome.

20 Subcomandante Marcos, quoted in Ana Carrigan, "Chiapas, the First Postmodern Revolution," in Subcomandante Insurgente Marcos, *our word is our weapon: selected writings*, ed. Juana Ponce de Leon (New York: Seven Stories Press, 2001), 417

21 Ibid., 427.

22 Clark's comment widely reported. See Ian Austin, Frank Luba, and Cheryl Chan, "B.C. Government to Seek Injunction against Occupy Vancouver," the *Vancouver Province*, November 22, 2011, A3. It is perhaps worth noting, in light of what I have argued about the containment of the Occupy movement at the municipal level, that while the "problem" of the occupation was still being pursued by the City of Vancouver, it extended here, briefly, to the provincial and federal levels, in so far as the legal action taken against the encampment.

23 A significant failure of Occupy Vancouver occurred when many homeless people were left with nowhere to go after the abandonment of the encampment. It's a failure, certainly, of the City, the system, and the society at large to properly deal with homelessness, but Occupy Vancouver activists, too, turned their backs on the homelessness issue.

24 David Harvey, *Spaces of Hope* (Berkeley: University of California Press, 2000).

25 The spokescouncil model is very effective for three reasons. First, it does not replace the GA as a decision-making body – what it does is take some of the structural information sharing and reporting weight off its shoulders, freeing the GA up for the decision-making process. Second, it allows everyone, according to their abilities, to participate transparently in the local/global dialectic (thus diversifying and disseminating opinions/views at all levels, and strengthening the movement through diversity and increased solidarity. Third, it is not a model of "representation" (with built-in problems of unequal and privilege-generating access to information/decision making) but one of extended participation (with a committee or subgroup's "spoke" being just that – a spokesperson for the group who must simply report on behalf of, and report back to, his or her committee or group, and whose position is rotating and temporary). See the Occupy Portland website for an excellent description of the spokescouncil model: http://www.portlandgeneralassembly.org /assemblies/spokescouncil-description.

26 I take this phrase from Matt Taibbi, "How I Stopped Worrying and Learned to Love the OWS Protests" *Rolling Stone*, November 10, 2011, http://www.rollingstone.com/politics/news/how-i-stopped-worrying-and-learned-to-love-the-ows-protests-20111110.

27 Michael Hardt and Antonio Negri. *Commonwealth* (Cambridge, MA: Belknap Press, 2009), 180.

28 Ibid., 184, 189.

29 Ibid., 196–97.

30 Don Hazen, "OWS: to Change the Country, We Just Might Have to Change Ourselves," alternet.org, November 21, 2011, http://www .alternet.org/story/153165/ows%3A_to_change_the_country,_we _just_might_have_to_change_ourselves_?page=entire.

31 I am in part riffing off a statement made by occupier Tosh Hyodo at an Occupy Vancouver working group meeting.

32 Klein was interviewed on December 1, 2011, by members of the Occupy Vancouver Media Committee. Ian MacKenzie's video of the interview can be found at the Occupy Vancouver Voice website (http://occupyvancouvervoice.com/naomi-klein-interview-with -occupy-vancouver/).

33 Karl Marx, *Capital: A Critique of Political Economy*, vol. 1., trans. Ben Fowkes (Harmondsworth: Penguin Books, 1976), 283.

34 David Harvey, *A Companion to Marx's "Capital"* (London: Verso, 2010), 112.

35 Andrew C. Revkin, "Naomi Klein's Inconvenient Climate Conclusions," *New York Times*, December 7, 2011, http://dotearth.blogs .nytimes.com/2011/12/07/naomi-kleins-inconvenient-climate -conclusions/.

36 John Bellamy Foster, "Capitalism and the Accumulation of Catastrophe," *The Monthly Review* 63, no. 7 (December 2011).

37 Marx, like many economists, is working from Aristotle in this regard. See the *Politics*, Book I, Chapters 8–9. See also James Bernard Quilligan's excellent analysis of this Aristotelian economic background in "Toward a Common Theory of Value, Part One: Common Being." *Kosmos* (Fall–Winter 2011): 37–43.

38 Also working from the C-M-C / M-C-M schematic, James Bernard Quilligan has argued, more eloquently and with a firmer understanding of economics, for a similar need to "make the economy a component part of the biosphere." See "Toward a Common Theory of Value: Part Two: Common Trust," *Kosmos* (Spring–Summer 2012): 56–62.

39 Derrick Penner, "Pipelines Will Fuel Plenty of Talk," *Vancouver Sun*, December 31, 2011, A6.

40 Barry Saxifrage, "Vancouver's 100-mile Carbon Hot Spots," *Vancouver Observer*, January 12, 2012, http://www.vancouver observer.com/blogs/climatesnapshot/2011/01/04/vancouver%E2% 80%99s-100-mile-carbon-hot-spots.

41 "Who Is Looking After Burrard Inlet?" Posted on Tsleil-Waututh First Nation website, November 22, 2011, www.twnation.ca.

42 Harsha Walia, "Decolonizing Together: Moving Beyond a Politics of Solidarity Toward a Practice of Decolonization," *Briarpatch Magazine*, January 1, 2012, http://briarpatchmagazine.com/articles/ view/decolonizing-together.

43 For more detailed data on Canadian exports, see Foreign Affairs and International Trade Canada, "Canada's State of Trade: Trade and Investment Update 2011," http://www.international.gc.ca/economist -economiste/performance/state-point/state_2011_point/SoT _2011_ToC.aspx?view=d.

44 $111 billion during the 2008/09 financial crisis. See "Canadian Bank Bailout Total Touches $186 billion," *Wellington Financial* (blog), December 2, 2010, http://www.wellingtonfund.com/blog/2010/12 /02/canadian-bank-bailout-total-touches-186-billion/#axzz20 WrgQQJ2.

45 Oliver's claims were made in an "open letter" published on the Mar-ketWatch page of the *Wall Street Journal* and widely reported in the media, January 9, 2012.

46 Supreme Court of British Columbia judgment, http://www.courts .gov.bc.ca/jdb-txt/SC/11/16/2011BCSC1647.htm [section 56].

47 Quoted in Gerald Raunig, *Art and Revolution: Transversal Activism in the Long Twentieth Century* (Los Angeles: Semiotext(e), 2007), 12.

48 Ibid., 17.

49 Ibid., 17–18.

50 Installed at the Vancouver Art Gallery's "Offsite" space, February 2–September 16, 2012.

51 Anthony D. Barnosky et al, "Approaching a State Shift in Earth's Biosphere," *Nature* 486 (June 2012): 52–58.

52 Graeber, *Debt*, 367.

53 Robert Kunzig, "Population 7 Billion," *National Geographic* (January 2011), http://ngm.nationalgeographic.com/2011/01/seven-billion/ kunzig-text.

54 Graeber, *Debt*, 386.

Part 3
Letter from Rome

1   Ammianus Marcellinus, *The Later Roman Empire*, quoted in John Burrow, *A History of Histories: Epics, Chronicles, Romances and Inquiries from Herodotus and Thucydides to the Twentieth Century* (London: Penguin, 2009), 159.

2   Quoted in Hanna Arendt, *On Revolution*, 244.

3   *¡Democracia Real YA!* is a Spanish grass-roots social movement that launched the May 2011 occupation of the Puerta del Sol in Madrid.

4   Robert Hughes, *Rome: A Cultural, Visual, and Personal History* (New York: Knopf, 2011), 169.

5   Jean-Jacques Rousseau, *The Social Contract*, trans. Maurice Cranston (London: Penguin Books, 1968 [1762]), 141.

6   Arendt, *On Revolution*, 31.

7   William L. MacDonald, *The Pantheon: Design, Meaning, and Progeny* (Cambridge, MA: Harvard University Press, 1976), 88.

8   Livy, *The Early History of Rome – Books I–V of The History of Rome from its Foundation*, trans. Aubrey De Sélincourt. (Baltimore: Penguin Books, 1960), 129.

9   Ibid., 137, 140.

10 Rousseau, *The Social Contract*, 113.

11 Fergus Millar, *The Roman Republic in Political Thought* (Hanover: University Press of New England, 2002), 30. *Polybius, The Histories* vol. 3, no. 3, trans. W.R. Paton (Cambridge, MA: Harvard University Press, 1923), 273.

12 Dimitis Christoulas's suicide note, as reported in *Athens News*, April 4, 2012.

13 Hughes, *Rome*, 82.

14 Walter Benjamin, "Theses on the Philosophy of History," in *Illuminations: Essays and Reflections*, ed. Hannah Arendt, trans. Harry Zohn (New York: Schocken Books, 1968), 256.

15 Burrow, *A History of Histories*, 96.

16 Polybius, *The Histories, Books 5–8*, rev. ed. (Cambridge, MA: Loeb Classical Library, 2011), 275, 289.

17 Ibid., 289.

18 Quoted in Hughes, *Rome*, 6.

19 I am largely relying upon Eric Chaisson here: *Cosmic Evolution: The Rise of Complexity in Nature* (Cambridge, MA: Harvard University Press, 2001).

20 MacDonald, *The Pantheon*, 85.

21 Ibid., 67.

22 Ibid., 88–89.

23 Ibid., 76.

24 This is Hippolytus's summary of Empedocles's views, from his *Refu-tation of All Heresies*. See Jonathan Barnes, *Early Greek Philosophy* (London: Penguin Books, 1987): 174, 195.

25 Jean-Pierre Vernant, *The Origins of Greek Thought* (Ithaca: Cornell University Press, 1982), 45.

26 Henry David Thoreau, "Resistance to Civil Government," in *Walden and Resistance to Civil Government*, ed. William Rossi (New York: Norton, 1966), 245.

27 Millar, *The Roman Republic in Political Thought*, 6.

28 Rousseau, *The Social Contract*, 112.

29 Millar, *The Roman Republic in Political Thought*, 6.

30 Harvey, *A Companion to Marx's "Capital"*, 112.

31 Peter J. Richerson and Robert Boyd, *Not by Genes Alone: How Culture Transformed Human Evolution* (Chicago: University of Chicago Press, 2005), 4. The rest of the passage is worth noting: "Culture and cultural change cannot be understood solely in terms of innate psychology. Culture affects the success and survival of individuals and groups; as a result, some cultural variants spread and others diminish, leading to evolutionary processes that are every bit as real and important as those that shape genetic varia-tion. These culturally evolved environments then affect which genes are favored by natural selection. Over the long haul, culture has shaped our innate psychology as much as the other way around."

32 Polybius and Appian cited in Burrow, *A History of Histories*, 69, 121.

33 L. Nathan Oaklander, *The Ontology of Time* (New York: Prometheus Books, 2004), 20.

34 Fredric Jameson, *Archaeologies of the Future: The Desire Called Utopia and Other Science Fictions* (London: Verso, 2005), xii.

35 Richerson and Boyd, *Not by Genes Alone*, 49–50.

36 Clive Ponting, *A New Green History of the World: The Environment and the Collapse of Great Civilizations*, rev. ed. (New York: Penguin, 2007), 37. Ponting compares this "ratchet effect" to a "feedback loop."

37 Ibid., 52.

38 Chaisson, *Cosmic Evolution*, 198.

39 Ibid., 196.

40 J. Donald Hughes. *An Environmental History of the World: Human-kind's Changing Role in the Community of Life* (London: Routledge, 2009), 188.

41 Ponting, *A New Green History of the World*, 414.

42 David Christian, *Maps of Time: An Introduction to Big History* (Berkeley: University of California Press, 2004), 506–11.

43 Chaisson, *Cosmic Evolution*, 16.

44 Christian, *Maps of Time*, 509.

45 Ibid., 80.

46 Chaisson, *Cosmic Evolution*, 199.

47 Ibid., 27.

48 Ponting, *A New Green History of the World*, 197.

49 Streeck, "The Crises of Democratic Capitalism," 5.

50 *The Letters of Sacco and Vanzetti*, eds., Marion Denman Frankfurter and Gardner Jackson (New York: Viking Press, 1928), 219.

51 Ibid., 219–20.

52 Ibid., 220.

53 Ibid., 222.

54 Daniel Dennett, *Freedom Evolves* (New York: Penguin Books, 2003), 10.

55 Ibid., 13.

56 Ibid., 157.

57 "A system has a degree of freedom when there is an ensemble of possibilities of one kind or another, and which of these possibilities is actual at any time depends on whatever function or switch controls this degree of freedom" (Dennett, *Freedom Evolves*, 162).

58 Dennett, *Freedom Evolves*, 53, 165.

59 David Harvey offers another version of the overdetermined complexity that sets the conditions for modern humanity and "provides strategic options for human action" – a "repertoire derived from evolutionary experience" which includes (but does not delimit the human to) "competition and the struggle for existence," "adaptation and diversification into environmental niches," "collaboration, cooperation and mutual aid," "environmental transformations (the transformation and modification of 'nature')," "spatial orderings" (the production of space), and "temporal orderings" (*Spaces of Hope*, 209). Harvey works up a theory of social change based on this matrix: "If capitalism cannot survive without deploying all of the repertoire in some way, then the task for socialism must be to find a different combination of all the elements from within the basic repertoire" (211).

60 Richerson and Boyd, *Not by Genes Alone*, 55–57.

61 Ibid., 74.

62 Ibid., 131–34.

63 Ibid., 138–39.

64 Ibid., 195.

65 Norman Doidge, *The Brain that Changes Itself: Stories of Personal Triumph from the Frontiers of Brain Science* (New York: Viking, 2007), 23.

66 Ibid., 203

67 Vernant, *The Origins of Greek Thought*, 11.

68 Ibid., 123.

69 Ibid., 122.

70 Ibid., 124.

71 The Invisible Committee, *The Coming Insurrection*, 6.

72 Karl Marx and Friedrich Engels, *The Communist Manifesto*, ed. L.M. Findlay (Peterborough, ON: Broadview Editions, 2004 [1848]), 80.

73 Harvey, *Spaces of Hope*, 203.

74 Alain Badiou, *The Communist Hypothesis*, trans. David Macey and Steve Corcoran (London: Verso, 2010), 256.

75 Harvey, *Spaces of Hope*, 195.

76 Ibid., 186.

77 Slavoj Žižec, *Violence: Six Sideways Reflections* (New York: Picador, 2008), 76.

78 Ibid., 77.

79 Ibid., 21.

80 Ibid., 18.

81 Ibid., 223–24.

82 Ibid., 249.

83 Robespierre's report to the Assembly on the rights of societies and clubs, September 29, 1791, as quoted in Arendt, 240.

84 Ibid., 262.

85 Ibid., 264–65.

86 On "rest in change," see G.S, Kirk's commentary on *Heraclitus in The Cosmic Fragments*, ed. G.S. Kirk (Cambridge: Cambridge University Press, 1962), 377.

87 Charles Eisenstein, "Debt and the Tar Sands," occupy.com, April 4, 2012, http://www.occupy.com/article/debt-and-tar-sands-0.

88 Marx, *Capital*, vol. 1, 875. Marx is here describing the process of "primitive accumulation," a key plank in the platform of which was the enclosure of the common lands.

89 David Graeber, *Debt: The First 5,000 Years* (Brooklyn: Melville House, 2011), 346.

90 Ibid., 385–86.

91 Ibid., 318–19: "What's more, that relationship [embodied in speculative colonizers like Cortes], between the daring adventurer on the one hand, the gambler willing to take any sort of risk, and on the

other, the careful financier, whose entire operations are organized around producing steady, mathematical, inexorable growth of income, lies at the heart of what we now call 'capitalism.'" Graeber later takes this a step further, noting "a deeper, more profound relation between gambling and apocalypse. Capitalism as a system that enshrines the gambler as an essential part of its operation, in a way that no other system ever has; yet at the same time, capitalism seems to be uniquely incapable of conceiving of its own eternity" (357). This is very much the essence of our current dilemma.

92 Ibid., 373.

93 Ibid., 376.

94 Ibid., 383.

95 Ponting, *A New Green History of the World*, 293. I am taking the term "transgenerational" thought from Spencer Wells, *Pandora's Seed: The Unforeseen Cost of Civilization* (New York: Random House, 2010), 58, 159.

96 Leo Goretti, "The Good, the Bad, and the Ugly: Notes on the Rome Riot," *Verso Books* (blog), October 25, 2011.

97 See Dennett, *Freedom Evolves*, 56.

98 Ethan Cox, "It Starts in Quebec: Our Revolution of Love, Hope and Community," rabble.ca, May 27, 2012.

Index

Stephen Collis is an award-winning poet, activist, and professor of contemporary literature at Simon Fraser University. His poetry books include *Anarchive* (New Star, 2005 – nominated for the BC Book Prize for Poetry), *The Commons* (Talonbooks, 2008), *On the Material* (Talonbooks, 2010 – awarded the BC Book Prize for Poetry), and the forthcoming *To the Barricades* (Talonbooks, 2013). He has also written two books of literary criticism and a forthcoming novel, *The Red Album* (BookThug, 2013). He lives in Tsawwassen, British Columbia.

OKANAGAN PUBLIC LIBRARY
3 3132 03373 4965